A New Teacher's Survival Guide:
Everything They Forgot To Tell You During Credentialing

You cannot teach anyone anything; you can
only help them find it within themselves.

Galileo

A New Teacher's Survival Guide: Everything They Forgot To Tell You During Credentialing

By
Mark Nicholas Remy

Siena Publishing
San Diego, California

A NEW TEACHER'S SURVIVAL GUIDE:
EVERYTHING THEY FORGOT TO
TELL YOU DURING CREDENTIALING

Published by: Siena Publishing
San Diego, CA
619-298-6717 Telephone and FAX
mremy@pwa.acusd.edu

All rights reserved. No part of this book may be reproduced, stored in a retrieval system, or transmitted, in any form or by any means, electronic, mechanical, photocopying, recording or otherwise, without permission in writing from the author and/or publisher. The only exceptions are forms and pages designated in the text by the author as reproducible for teacher use.

Copyright © 1997 by Mark Nicholas Remy

Printed in the United States of America
First Printing, 1997

Cover and Book Design by Mark Nicholas Remy and Aric Von Henschen
Photographs by Mark Nicholas Remy

Library of Congress Cataloging in Publication Data
Remy, Mark Nicholas
      A New Teacher's Survival Guide:
Everything They Forgot To Tell You During Credentialing

1. Classroom management
2. Education, Elementary
3. Discipline, elementary school
4. Academic achievement
5. Pedagogy
I. Title

Library of Congress Catalog Card Number 97-92217
ISBN 0-9659349-1-8

DEDICATIONS

Special thanks to Dr. Virgil Blanke, Keith Canova, Ramona Adams Remy and Erin Tyler for their many hours of proofreading and editing; to Mark Heinze, Patricia Parks, Jodie Roberts, Matt Shirley and, again Virgil for their kind words which evolved into endorsements; to Dr. Jon Lovette for enduring endless questions about the mechanics of publishing; to Rena Krekler for lending her photographic expertise; to Aric Von Henschen for graphic art design work and to all my students, past and present, who made this book possible by being *my* teachers.

TABLE OF CONTENTS

CHAPTER		PAGE
	Introduction	1
I.	Classroom Environment	3
II.	Life Outside Of The School Site: Do Not Over Extend Yourself:	15
III.	Classroom Organization	19
IV.	The Line	29
V.	Attendance	33
VI.	Discipline: The Card System	37
VII.	Classroom Helpers	43
VIII.	How To Communicate Effectively: Saying More By Saying Less	59
IX.	Homework Collection	67
X.	Desk Arrangement	75

XI.	Start The Day Patriotically	81
XII.	Opening Activities: Calendar, Ones-Tens-Hundreds and Weather	87
XIII.	Parent Letter Home	97
XIV.	Academic and Weekly Behavior Report	103
XV.	Acquiring Resources	107
XVI.	Your Teaching Aide	111
XVII.	Tips To Staying Healthy	115
XVIII.	Student Behavior: My Ten Best Tips	121
XIX.	Finances	125

INTRODUCTION

At some point you decided, "I want to be a teacher." Teaching is one of the noblest professions. To see a student learn and grow satisfies more than words can express. You have touched another life and it will never be the same. Henry B. Adams, a well known educator and writer, once commented, "A teacher affects eternity; he can never tell, where his influence stops."

The profession is, also, one of the most demanding, fatiguing, frustrating and overwhelming. A good teacher must learn methods or strategies to cope effectively. Do not allow certain factors to detract from the rewards of teaching. A balance must be found which creates a conduit to student achievement, to teacher satisfaction and to coping with daily minutia.

This book recounts lessons learned from my last three years as an elementary school teacher and from those of others who were once first year teachers. In retrospect, I wish someone would have sat me down and given me common sense advice on what to do and not to do my first year. Student achievement and citizenship would have been enhanced, lessons more focused and effectively planned and teacher anxiety, fatigue and frustration reduced. This book will help you with much of the nuts and bolts of getting started in the teaching profession. I see it as a supplement to the process of teacher accreditation through the Credentialing Program. Follow its lead, and your first year will be easier, less stressed, more enjoyable and ultimately better for your students. The first chapter discusses a teaching philosophy that creates a productive and nurturing classroom environment.

CHAPTER 1
CLASSROOM ENVIRONMENT

Every classroom has a unique learning environment. The teacher creates this environment by establishing a certain tone. I define "tone" as clear and consistent rules, firm but fair discipline, well defined, challenging and achievable expectations of what the teacher requires from students, well planned and organized lessons taught in a contextually clear manner, in-class assignments and homework with concise and understandable directions, constant time-on-task and keeping promises (teachers and students). Tone, as defined [above], is my underlying philosophy for creating rapport between teachers and students. If a teacher has rapport and a strong relationship with his/her students anything is possible.

Recently, a student was transferred to my class. It was the third transfer in less than three months. The student's two prior teachers complained about low assignment completion, poor citizenship and a general lack of participation. From the first day, I refused to accept these behavior patterns. I established a positive, encouraging and motivating relationship with the student. As a result, the student does not exhibit any of the prior behavior patterns. Assignments are completed and handed in on time, citizenship/behavior has been superb and participation continues to increase and improve. I was even informed, via another teacher, that the student was very happy with my class. Why did I achieve success when others failed? I have rapport and a strong relationship with the student. How did I establish it? That will be the topic of discussion in the following sections.

Clear and Consistent Rules

On the first day of the new school year in September, I clearly and concisely explain my classroom rules. They are few, but cover what is required in the area of behavior. Additionally, keep all rules in the affirmative. Refrain from using words like "Don't" or "No" (for example: "Don't run, No talking, No yelling out, etc.). The following are my general rules:

1. **Raise your hand before speaking.**
2. **Be responsible for your actions.**
3. **Arrive on time and be seated before the bell rings.**
4. **Follow directions.**
5. **Work quietly and in your assigned seat or work area.**
6. **Always do the best work possible.**

As adults, we prefer to know what is required of us. When the rules are clear and boundaries defined, life is much easier. When the rules arbitrarily change, are undefined or non-existent, we feel unsure of our actions and do not accomplish tasks with the same degree of success. This is also true for children. When they know what is expected of them and what they can expect from their teacher, a positive and mutually supportive relationship develops. Students work harder, complete assignments with higher standards, behave better, are more responsible for their actions and attend school with a greater desire to learn.

Firm But Fair Discipline

A classroom without discipline will be a less than effective learning environment. The teacher must establish certain boundaries within the classroom. I feel it is necessary to have a highly disciplined learning environment. In part, this centers on my conversation in the last section about clear and consistent rules. However, rules are useless if they are neither enforced nor applied equally to all. Teachers can not apply certain rules to students that are behavior problems and look the other way when a usually well-behaved or favorite student commits an infraction. This sends a bad message to students. "If I am good most of the time the teacher will not punish me when I break a rule." This can also escalate into increased infractions by your well-behaved students.

Furthermore, your students that break rules realize that there is little they can do to improve. They accept punitive action and may even become conditioned to acquiring negative attention through these actions. My advice is to treat all equally, apply rules judiciously and follow through on all consequences administered. Do not play favorites. If a good student fails to complete his/her homework they stay in at recess, just as would a student that consistently fails to complete homework. Firm, but fair discipline compliments clear and concise rules. Remember, students work better in a well defined, disciplined and structured classroom environment. If you know what is expected, you will accomplish the task with greater ease and higher standards.

Well Defined, Challenging and Achievable Expectations

Students will always rise to the expectations set by the teacher. Set high standards in all areas and accept only work satisfying your academic demands. Self-esteem increases exponentially with assignment completion and high standards. Students are cognizant of a job well-done and understand that hard work creates a quality product.

If I require a journal entry of an entire page, with accurate spelling, grammatically complete sentences, punctuation and a well developed theme, my students comply. It is understood that I will not accept less than what is required. If they do not comply, they complete the assignment during recess or after school.

Special note: forfeited recess is the best leverage for exacting behavior modification. Elementary students love recess and will do almost anything for it. Let your students know that recess is an earned privilege, a reward for studious behavior and not a right that goes without sacrifice. Please check with your district office prior to implementing this intervention. There might be regulations prohibiting it.

Well Planned And Organized Lessons Taught In A Contextually Clear Manner

Throughout the entire book, I stress the importance of planning and organization. In this section, I target the necessity for well-planned and organized lessons taught in a contextually clear manner. I will not discuss what constitutes a well-planned and organized lesson. That in itself should be clear after the credentialing process and student teaching. However, lessons taught in a contextually clear manner needs definition.

What do I mean by "in context"? The other day, I was at the supermarket. I saw a mother with a baby. The baby had started to talk and was saying daddy and mommy and several other words. The mother picked up a loaf of bread and the baby said, "daddy." The mother held the bread in front of the baby, allowed him to touch it and said, "bread, this is bread, bread." After several attempts the baby repeated, "bed," "red" and finally "bread." I saw this as a successful lesson taught in a contextually clear manner. The baby understood that daddy was not the correct word. Furthermore, the mother gave the baby a visual prompt (the loaf of bread), a clear and repetitive auditory response, an opportunity to touch the bread and adequate time to process what had been seen, heard and touched. The end result was the baby's willing and successful attempt to learn a new word, contextually. By using sight, touch, hearing and speech the word "bread" was added to the baby's long-term memory. When bread is thought of in the future, a mental picture will appear, reinforcing and clarifying the meaning of the word while triggering an auditorily correct response.

Teach your lessons in the same manner. The concept conveyed should be placed in an understandable format that promotes long-term memory gain, retention and readily available use. Enable your students to use multiple senses to grasp meaning, send a clear message about what is being taught, and ultimately how to use that information. Teaching in a contextually clear manner will serve your students well and make your lessons powerful.

Clear and Understandable In-Class Assignments and Homework

In-class assignments and homework without clear and well explained directions will create unprecedented amounts of frustration. If a student does not understand what needs to be done, how can they complete an assignment? Furthermore, if a connection between the assignment and what should be learned is not evident, student interest declines. Assign meaningful work with clear instructions. Explain why it is important and how this knowledge is transferable to other activities. Tell your students that they will use this information for the rest of their life.

Every week, my students are assigned fifteen (15) new vocabulary words. The words promote a greater understanding of the English language, enhance writing skills and aide more fluid reading capabilities. One weekly activity includes putting the fifteen (15) words in alphabetical order. Students use this skill to look-up words in dictionaries, find phone numbers in the yellow pages and even sort student files by last name. They make a connection why alphabetical order is important and useful in daily life.

I also recommend assigning homework each week that follows the same format. For example:

Monday: One page dictation in journal.

Tuesday: Wordfind introducing fifteen (15) new vocabulary words and words placed in alphabetical order.

Wednesday: Students read aloud to parents and parents sign a confirmation sheet of homework completion.

Thursday: All vocabulary words are written ten times each in preparations for Friday's spelling quiz.

Friday: All words spelled incorrectly on the quiz are written five times each and turned in on Monday.

This homework routine has several advantages. First, students clearly understand what is expected and how to complete assignments. Second, parents know exactly what homework to look for and check every night. This garners support from parents and increases chances of parent participation. Thirdly, teachers are able to prepare well targeted homework indicative of the needs of a student population and to fine tune it through repeated use.

Constant Time-On-Task

I can not impress upon teachers the importance of time-on-task. I firmly believe that every minute in the classroom must be utilized in a productive manner. Have well planned lessons, be organized and prepared to start as soon as the students arrive. Do not waste time, allowing students to sit idle. They want to work and learn. I keep my students on-task using many of the strategies discussed in this book.

Keeping Promises

Many years ago, my mother told me to never make a promise I was not willing to keep. Promises should be honored. They build one's credibility. Credibility lays a firm foundation in the area of trust, respect, consistency, rapport and friendship. Teachers lose a great deal of respect when they fail to fulfill a promise. For example, if I tell my students we will go on a field trip, I make it happen. I keep my promise. They learn that they can count on me and that my word is my bond. Additionally, you model a strong character trait which transfers to your students. They will understand the intrinsic value of keeping one's promises and building integrity with others. In the classroom, students should know what is expected from the teacher and the teacher from the students.

Recess

While having this book critiqued, several fellow educators expressed concern about the loss of recess as an intervention for better citizenship, behavior modification or as a time to complete homework and/or in-class assignments. In many districts, it is illegal to deprive students of recess. It is considered a time to drink water, use the bathroom, get exercise, integrate with diverse ethnicities and just take a break. Before depriving a student of recess, either rarely or consistently, please consider getting parental permission in the form of a signed waiver. Personally, I have always given parents prior notice, requesting permission in writing, over the telephone or in person. Additionally, check with your district office to learn what the specific regulations are regarding a student's recess.

If you are permitted to use recess as an intervention, please, allow your student(s) a chance to use the bathroom and water fountain around the time recess usually occurs. The loss of recess should not be torture! If a student fails to complete an assignment under "normal" conditions, imagine what the probability of assignment completion will be if a student is thirsty or in dire need of the bathroom.

The Room Itself: Walls and Windows

Almost every classroom will be comprised of walls and windows. There are a few exceptions where rooms have no windows and some walls are partitions or moveable sectioned wall units. However, for the most part you will have walls and windows in your classroom.

I can not impress upon you enough, the importance of having a print rich environment. How do I define "print rich." The walls are covered with useful information that students look at, absorb, refer to during assignments, question, read and most importantly from which they learn. The following are examples of material I always place on my walls:

Signs depicting North, South, East and West

Posters with verb conjugations for "to have," "to want," "to need," "to be," and "to go" in the present, past and future

Positive affirmation banners:
"There is nothing like a dream to create the future."
Victor Hugo
"What we have to learn to do, we learn by doing."
Aristotle

A list of all the books we have read as a class

My district's Academic Standards

A calendar and weather station

Varied maps of the world, countries, U.S., and California

Posters of pictures from around the world

The alphabet in manuscript and printed

"The Star Spangled Banner" for daily singing

The five food groups in poster form (Nutrition)

Bulletin boards and clothes lines with student work

This next recommendation may seem to beleaguer the obvious; however, I will state it all the same. If you have windows, please open them. I know that weather permitting and your windows' functioning ability to open may dictate how much and how often you open them, but open them as much as possible. Additionally, some windows may be hard to open or take a little extra time. Invest the energy and time. Every morning, I spend five minutes opening my top windows with a window extension bar. It is difficult, physically exerting and takes precision motor skills (I can not tell you how many times I almost put the window extension bar through a pane of glass). My premise is **your students need a plentiful and consistent source of fresh air.** I can not tell you how many times I have gone into a classroom with stale air that was filled with a stench. Fresh air keeps students alert and awake. Assist them with what I consider a basic necessity - - - oxygen!

The Room Itself: Keep It Tidy

I am very organized. I prefer to know where everything is and be able to get at it within seconds. Over the years, teachers, parents, aides, administrators and students have come into my room and commented on how organized everything was maintained. Not everyone needs to be as obsessive or compulsive as I am. However, I fervently recommend putting things in the same place and in a neat orderly fashion. You will infrequently waste time looking for needed materials. Students will always know where to go to get a pencil, ruler, dictionary, paper, journal, etc. Additionally, a clean, tidy and well organized room sends a strong message to your students. Personally, I feel that it reinforces and models my standards; it visually sets a standard in the area of doing neat, organized and well thought-out/developed work. The following are several examples of how I keep my room organized, neat and tidy.

My Best Suggestions

Use metal or plastic tiered paper holders

Have all books neatly arranged in book cases

Adjust all vertical blinds to the same height

Use my box system for pencils, homework and notices home (Ch. 3)

Place all posters, charts, banners, etc. in an esthetically pleasant arrangement. Do not let them be crooked! Hang them with another person that can tell you up a little, to the left a little, etc.

Ensure that your desks are straight, aligned and in their correct position

If your handwriting is less than desirable, (as is mine), get someone with neat, legible handwriting to write out your signs, banners, charts, etc. Personally, I prefer to do as much as possible on a computer.

When finished with the blackboard or whiteboard, erase it. Wash your blackboard frequently. Chalk dust build-up will make any room messier.

If a room is especially messy after a project have the students sweep the floor. I usually have more volunteers to sweep than brooms. The room is their home away from home. Students prefer to take part in its cleanliness. Additionally, others will scrub desks. I keep rags and a mild liquid cleaner provided by my Custodians.

Maintain clean desks. Have students clean-out desks every week. It is amazing what will gather inside of them. This will also help you recover lost rulers, pencils, scissors, library books, erasers, etc.

Many other examples exist. Add them to the list as you become more and more organized, tidy and neat.

CHAPTER 2

LIFE OUTSIDE OF THE SCHOOL SITE: DO NOT OVER EXTEND YOURSELF

Your first year will be a busy one. The energy expended to just keep on top of everything will be exhausting. Attempt not to take on too much. What do I mean by too much? The following are several examples:

Example One: Degrees

Don't start another degree such as a specialized Teaching Credential (SED, Spec. Ed., G.A.T.E., Etc.), Masters, or even a Doctorate. Degrees are taxing mentally, physically and emotionally. They are designed to allow a student to grow intellectually, i.e. learn. Additionally, having to do papers, presentations, intern/student teaching hours and attending class will reduce time and energy necessary for lesson preparation and effective instruction.

I advocate degree advancement. You can never have too much education! I am currently a doctoral student in Educational Leadership. The degree will exponentially increase opportunities in the field of education. However, to do this during the first or even second year is physical and mental suicide. I finished my Teaching Credential during my first year of Public School teaching and started my doctorate during my second. Those years were difficult. I was fortunate that by my second year I had acquired a teaching position at a superb Elementary School. Students wanted to learn, behavior problems were minimal, school services were very effective, parent support was second to none, Administration was approachable and responsive, and the teaching staff and my aide were experienced and helpful. These assets made coping with a "full plate" far more palatable. Not all teaching positions will afford you these luxuries. I strongly recommend waiting three or four years before initiating another credential or degree.

Example Two: Marriage

Many teachers decide that they will get married during their first year of teaching. They finally have a good job, are earning more money and want to settle down. I have seen several teachers who decided to get married and plan a wedding during their first year. In almost every case, it was a disaster emotionally and physically. A wedding is a very special event. The teachers with whom I have spoken all told me that to have waited another year would have been far more prudent. The wedding would have been more enjoyable and all the events during planning less fatiguing.

Example Three: Buying A House

To buy a house is part of the American dream. However, it is something else that I would not recommend for a teacher during the first year or two. The entire process of looking for a property, making an offer, a counter offer, escrow, closing, moving, setting-up a new home and many other details is exhausting. If home life is not secure, comfortable and stable, the work site becomes more stressed and difficult in general. Wait a few years, save some money, shop around and start the process when you have more time, energy and familiarity with work obligations.

These are only three examples. Many more exist that can arise during the first year of teaching. My premise is that to be stretched too thin, between too many activities will complicate your work site activities. You will need all the energy and focus possible to complete a fulfilling and successful year. Be a teacher and very little else your first year. It makes a huge difference in the classroom. Now that you have decided to focus on teaching, let's talk about organization in the classroom.

Notes . .

CHAPTER 3
CLASSROOM ORGANIZATION

I can not stress too fervently or enough the importance of being organized in the classroom and especially in front of the students. In my opinion, it is the key to being an effective, organized and respected educator. You will never be a successful teacher without meticulously planning and organizing in advance of entering the classroom.

Over the years, I have watched teachers instruct students. A well-planned lesson sends a clear message to students about what learning objective is desired, as opposed to a lesson with little or no planning, which sends an obscure message about what and how the teacher wants students to learn. You can not teach in an environment of little to no planning. Your principal, vice principal, fellow teachers, parents and especially students will notice. Everyone watches and notices what is going on (or not going on) in your classroom. Students miss very little. They see right through you; your facade is crystalline.

I recount the story about the day I got a new watch band. It was almost exactly the same as the old one: same color, design, band width, etc. I was not in my class thirty minutes before three different students noticed my new band and commented on it. If something as subtle as a watch band was noticed, imagine what they see in your lessons. They miss nothing. The following are some practical applications and examples of why organization and planning are so important.

Behavior

Many behavior problems result from students being off- task. If students do not understand what is expected of them, how can they initiate or even complete an assignment? Off-task behavior will result. Students never cease to amaze me. They will do massive amounts of work, as long as they know what needs to be done. A teacher that is organized with well-planned lessons will send a clearer message to the students, who in turn will better understand what is expected. A good teacher is able to explain what needs to be accomplished and how, and to get the vast majority of the students on-task during the first explanation. There will always be a few students that need a little extra help. This is normal. If we think of ourselves, there are numerous times when we, as adults, need a second or even a third explanation.

Know The Subject Matter

Planning also promotes more thorough knowledge about the subject matter taught. A teacher that stands in front of a class, without a good understanding of the curriculum sends an inferior message to the students. They will not listen intently, nor ask questions. Neither will they be receptive to information that promotes understanding and achievement. Sometimes when students do not learn, the teacher is not teaching. Too many times, I have seen teachers put out information that is inaccurate, incomplete or just wrong. You will never know everything about what you are teaching. If a question is asked and you don't know the answer, tell the students, "I don't know; however, I will find out and get back to you." Make sure you follow through. If you do not, your students will remind you. My point in this paragraph is to be well prepared and knowledgeable.

Weekly Lesson Planners

Every year my school district provides a weekly lesson plan book. It enables me to plan my lessons for an entire year. I have seen several over the years, but prefer the ELAN Publishing Company's weekly lesson plan book, edition W 208, forty weeks. They are based out of Meredith, N.H. 03253. I suggest you use this to plan and record lessons, activities, field trips, assemblies, meetings, conferences, emergency drills (fire, disaster or earthquake) and any other notable events needed to be remembered.

In the planner, I clearly divide my lessons by subject and time period. I allow for plenty of space to write as much or as little as necessary for a clear understanding of my lessons. Your lessons are not only being written for you, but also for your principal, vice principal, substitute or any observers. When they look at your planning book, they must be able to discern the lesson being taught and understand what and how the students will learn the lesson. I also suggest that you always have at least three weeks of lessons planned in advance. It gives lessons more vision. Each week should build off the prior weeks. Knowledge and learning is not separated into neat, clean cut packages, to be taught, stored and forgotten. All that is learned increases a better understanding of the big picture and greater whole that is life.

During the first year, you will probably think, "How can I make plans for three weeks when I can barely make plans for several days?" Do your best and try it. You will be pleasantly surprised how one week will flow into the next. Students will also notice that knowledge learned weeks earlier is still valuable, useful and incorporated into current lessons. Repetition and reinforcement will also increase memory retention. My point in this section is to use a weekly planner effectively with a developed vision of using knowledge acquired in the past during present and future lessons.

Between the back cover and the last page of my Elan planner, I always put a manila file folder labeled "Daily Things To Do." In this folder, I place all incoming memos, notices, forms, etc., which need some sort of action or response. Additionally, once completed, I either put them back in the folder for quick and easy access, deliver them to the appropriate destination or dispose of them if no longer needed. I always know where something is and am able to deliver it ASAP. You will receive an inordinate amount of paperwork as a teacher. Keep it organized, know where it is, complete it ASAP and return it ASAP. Do not let it get backed-up or overdue. It can become an enormous problem. Additionally, I strongly recommend making copies of the more important documentation. Paperwork can be misplaced or lost; a copy will expedite resubmission with increased expediency and reduced redundancy of a task you already completed.

Grade Books

During my first year, I recorded grades on sheets I once used while teaching classes at the university level. They worked adequately with tests, mid-terms and finals; however, with elementary and secondary students, I felt they were cumbersome and awkward. From my second year to the present, I acquired a standard grade book. It enabled me to record grades for the entire year, to avoid constantly putting new names in when a sheet became full, to keep all pages/grades assembled in one neat package and to look far more professional should someone request to see my grades. I recommend Hammond & Stephens Class Record Book,

10 Week Quarter, Form 635. They are based out of Fremont Nebraska 68025 (800-228-9875). This grade book is compact, durable, organized, practical and very professional looking.

Homework, Pencil and Notices Home Boxes

Part of being organized is knowing where all materials are located and keeping them within a moments reach. Homework, pencils and notices home are consistent daily items requiring prompt attention. I keep these materials separated, organized and prepared for distribution with a box system.

As demonstrated in the photograph above, I place three box lids from photocopy paper boxes on the window sill shelf. Each is clearly labeled, "Homework," "Pencils" and "Notices Home." At the beginning of the day, I place all homework received from my students in the *Homework Box*. This way all homework is in one quickly accessible area. When it is time to correct or review it, I know exactly where to go. It also reduces clutter on my desk. On an average day, I receive over one hundred pieces of homework. That can and will fill-up your desk.

In addition to collecting homework, I dispense it everyday. In the *Notices Home Box*, I place my homework for that day and any other notices that need to be sent home with the students. I receive frequent notices for parents. As they arrive throughout the course of the day, I place them in my *Notices Home Box*. Depending on the day and upcoming activities, I will receive a substantial amount of paperwork from the main office. The *Notices Home Box* keeps it organized and all in one place. During the last ten minutes of class, I go to my *Notices Home Boxes* and distribute all contents via Table Captains. In chapter seven, Table Captain duties are discussed in detail.

I maintain a *Pencil Box* for several reasons. First, I feel it is my responsibility to provide pencils to all my students, if they are unable to provide them for themselves. Second, pencil points will break. If students were permitted to sharpen pencils every time one broke, the pencil sharpener would be grinding incessantly. I find this far too disruptive. Some students will even break pencils purposely in order to get up, draw attention to themselves, disrupt and bother others and play in general. Additionally, the life of the pencil is reduced at a far too rapid rate.

By maintaining a *Pencil Box*, pencils are sharpened at the close of each day, waiting at-the-ready for the subsequent day's use by students who need a pencil or a replacement due to breakage or loss. The distractions of pencil sharpening is eliminated, disruptive behavior is reduced and the duration of pencil life is increased. Chapter 7 discusses Pencil Helper duties and how they compliment the use of a *Pencil Box*.

Important Daily Occurrences: Remember Them !

Throughout the course of the school day, I am bombarded by little things to remember which are out of the ordinary routine or pop up at the last minute. I called it the "daily minutia." If you attempt to keep all these little things in your head, you will forget something. I guarantee it! I have a system which, when employed consistently and effectively, will keep all "little-things-to-do or remember" organized effortlessly.

Select an area of your blackboard or whiteboard for the daily minutia. As something comes in to do (be it via a person, note, memo, pass, etc.) write it on the board in that preassigned area. Make sure you write who must report (names), what time and where they need to go or do (office, auditorium, field trip, student council, etc.). Additionally, there will always be those that forget a piece of documentation sent home, requiring a signature (Academic/Behavior Reports, field trip permission slips, etc.). Every week, I have my "Academic/Behavior Report" list on the board. I place the names of those that forgot to bring the Report. The following morning, I have a quick reference list. I check it and ask those students for their Reports. It also makes students aware that **I will not forget**. As an event occurs, or a person brings me documentation, I erase the event or name from the board. The following are several examples of how I remember the daily minutia.

Examples of Daily Minutia

Counseling Center 10:15 AM
Field Trip Orientation
Bobby, Sally, Jorge and Eva

Auditorium 1:30 PM
Student Council Meeting
Jonathan, Stacey and Paul

Academic/Behavior Report
Jimmy	Judy
Diego	Alex

Field Trip Permission Slips
Mario	Mary
Tim	Michael

Routines

Humans love to know what to expect. Some surprises are pleasant; however, the vast majority of surprises are a burden, stressful and even terrifying. I recently learned of a friend who lost his job. The loss came as a surprise and a shock. He and his wife were now forced to rethink finances, housing and job options. This surprise was not pleasant. This may seem extreme; however, its magnitude parallels surprises that students encounter in the class. A drastic and sudden change/surprise in the classroom can be devastating. For example, if a teacher decides to change the recess schedule by moving it back thirty minutes and reducing it by five minutes. The student's disappointment and anxiety is no less than that experienced by my adult friend.

This change impacts on how a student stays on-task, how much is completed, and how much is learned and retained. The student was used to working for two hours on Language Arts. At the end of two hours the student felt fatigued mentally, needed to stretch and basically take a break. Maybe the student was accustomed to using the bathroom during recess, now he/she must wait an additional half-an-hour. This alone could reduce focus, attention span and concentration. Two hours was also the perfect amount of time to complete assignments. Now you are left with an extra half-an-hour and students are left with nothing to do. The list could go on. The underlying premise is that a routine adds certainty and reduces apprehension and, thus, ultimately allows your students to learn and accomplish more by knowing what to expect.

Students love to accomplish assignments, please their teacher and be busy learning. Set a routine and stick with it. If it needs modification, modify it, but tell your students what is going to happen and why. They will understand and adapt with greater acceptance. The next chapter commences with the first of many successfully implemented routines. They have been tested, refined and proven to help students achieve better and learn more during an academic year.

CHAPTER 4
THE LINE

Most elementary schools start with a short period of recess in the morning. This usually takes place directly before the first bell and the commencement of the school day. When the first bell rings signaling students to line up, this marks the beginning of the day. It is essential that the day begins on a positive, upbeat note. The line is very important because it is the class' first contact as a whole group. If those first moments are positive, without any sort of conflict resulting, the entire day will go much smoother. Let's define a problematic line that creates difficulties for the teacher through the morning and pose a solution.

When the bell rings, students start running to their assigned area where their line forms. There will be many bodies in the same area with high energy levels, having just finished recess and excited about another day of school with their teacher and friends. The line forms, cutting takes place, touching and pushing occurs, words are exchanged, some have not stopped playing and the line is less than straight. This is typical. Can problems result from a situation like the one described above? Absolutely!

I have seen name calling, angry and heated discussions and even fights result from lines forming in this manner. Nor will these problems disappear as soon as the students enter the classroom. Most likely they will persist and influence student behavior and learning. A student that is angry, frustrated, scared, worried, nervous, etc. will not be at his/her best academically. Imagine two students who while lining up, get into an argument with each other that results in threats of a fight after school. The two students, and possible others that will be spectators, will be very preoccupied with the events to come. These students will neither concentrate nor learn much. We need to ask, "Why did this happen, and how can we find a solution?" Both have the same answer. The teacher was not outside two or three minutes before the first bell rang.

When a teacher is waiting for his/her students prior to the first bell, the tone and composure of the line is very different. Students are more responsible for their actions. I find that students not only form-up in straighter lines with less pushing, cutting, talking and other undesirable activities, but, also, arrive in the classroom sooner and are primed mentally to start the day. They understand that recess is over, and now it is time to learn. The underlying premise of this chapter is simple. Be outside two or three minutes prior to the first bell or at any other time that your class will be lining up. It sends a clear message that recess is over, and it is time to be academic. The few minutes you sacrifice on a daily basis will reduce hours of frustrating and difficult student behavior. In the next chapter, we will discuss how to accurately and efficiently take attendance.

Notes . .

CHAPTER 5
ATTENDANCE

Taking accurate and complete attendance is very important. If a student is not present, the office must be informed. Teachers provide this initial source of information. Additionally, the school will require a reason. Most of the time, absences result from sickness, doctor appointments, travel, inclement weather, personal emergencies or truancy. At most schools, the attendance secretary will handle calls home and any other eventuality that may occur due to a student's absence. Your primary obligation, as a teacher, is to send an accurate attendance roster to the office.

For three years, I have used a system which quickly and accurately allows me to find out who is present and absent. Every student in my class has an oaktag card with his/her name written on it. The card is usually three to five inches long and two inches high. I prefer to use cut up sentence strips. These cards are kept in a sentence strip holder, attached to one of my bulletin boards. As the students enter the class, directly after first bell, they go to the sentence strip holder and turn their name over. Stress the importance, to all students, that turning-over someone else's card is not acceptable. They turn-over their card and **ONLY** their card.

The entire class goes through this procedure in less than three minutes. My classes have always numbered between 28 and 35 students. All I need to do is look for the names still showing and do a quick classroom scan to verify. For example in the photograph below, Mariana's, Francisco's and Ramiro's cards have not been turned-over. I now know they are absent.

Several notes about the set-up of this system. First, besides putting names on the cards, also put student numbers on them. I give every student a number. It is theirs for the entire year. If I have thirty students, they will be ordered alphabetically by last name and then numbered 1 through 30. Throughout the course of the year, I will gain and lose students. This will throw-off the numbers correlated alphabetically, but by only four or five students. In chapter five, I will discuss the importance of numbers in greater detail.

Second, stress the importance of regular attendance to your students. You can not learn, if you are absent! At the top of the sentence strip holder, I have a summative statement about attendance. Woody Allen once said, "80% of success is showing up." This is true. The sign is there, they see it everyday and have it reinforced by my comments about repeated perfect daily attendance. Tell them that it makes you happy to see everyone, be enthusiastic about their presence and get them hooked on the praise they receive for being there and ready to learn. This philosophy makes a huge difference in daily attendance, student achievement and overall desire to learn.

Lastly, I teach more than just academic subjects. I teach responsibility, team work and importance of community within a classroom. Students start my daily routine with attendance. They know that everyday they are responsible for turning over their name card. Furthermore, this is only one of several duties they have within the classroom. I am in charge of the classroom, but relinquish certain activities, that teach responsibility, build team work and increase community in the class. **I firmly believe that a teacher's responsibility is to set the agenda and teach; and the students' is to learn, do their work and not distract others. However, students must have a certain degree of control over their environment. Never stifle students. So much potential is lost.** This is only one of several ways that I allow students to take charge of the class. In the next chapter, I will clearly explain the duties of my classroom helpers.

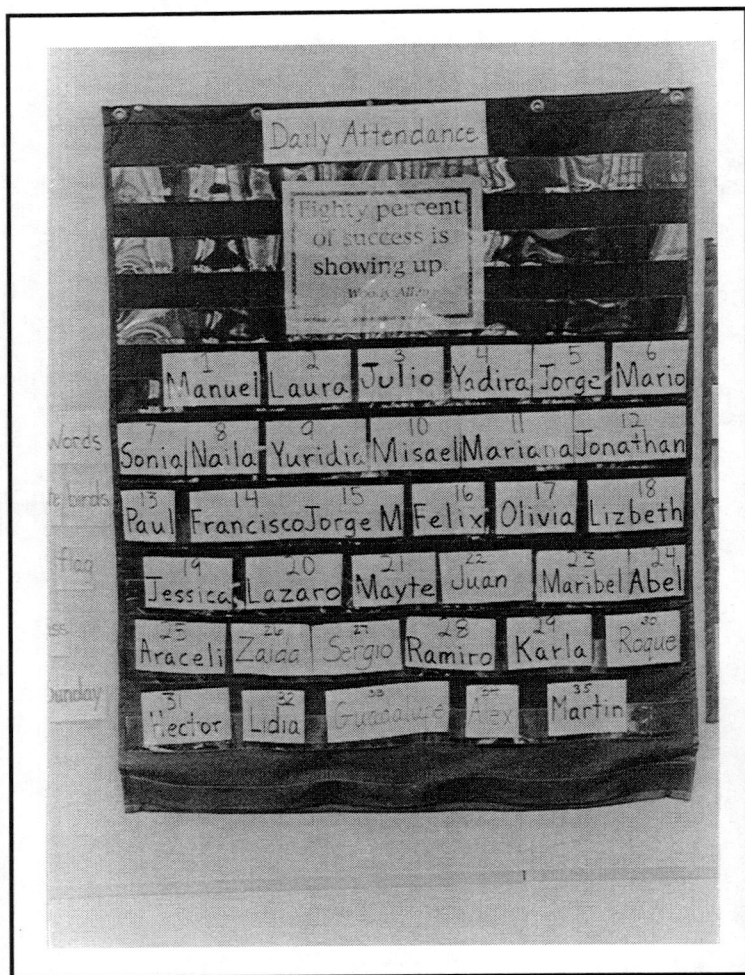

CHAPTER 6
DISCIPLINE: THE CARD SYSTEM

In chapter one, I discussed my general teaching philosophy. One of my primary premises is the need for firm, but fair discipline with consistent rules, consequences and rewards. At my elementary school, it is an unwritten rule that all classrooms use the card system.

The card system is set up as demonstrated in the photograph on page 38. A monthly calendar pocket chart is the best. There are usually thirty-five separate little pockets where the cards fit. In each pocket there are four different colored cards. I use green, pink, yellow and red cards, in that progression, to discipline students when an infraction is committed. The actual use of the system is simple. Each student has an assigned number. Written on each of the pockets of the card system chart are all student numbers. When an infraction is committed the teacher will instruct the student to go to the chart, locate their numbered pocket and turn a card. In each pocket, there are four cards in the green, pink, yellow and red progression. Each pocket commences with a green card which represents outstanding behavior with no infractions. After the first infraction is committed, the student will have a pink card showing in their pocket. If subsequent infractions are committed, the student will progress to yellow and then to red. Students always turn their own cards. I prefer that they accept responsibility for their own actions.

The entire process of being caught, getting-up, walking over to the card chart, turning a card and returning to their assigned seat sends a clear message that the behavior was inappropriate and must stop. In addition, the process affords students an opportunity to interrupt the inappropriate behavior pattern and get back on task. Furthermore, the teacher does not waste valuable instruction time. All that need be said is "_____(student's name), please turn a card." It is quick, efficient, consistent, fair and sends a clear message to stop misbehaving and get back on-task.

Each colored card, after green, needs a consequence. Without consequences, the cards possess no significance. I can only suggest consequences. Yours should mirror the discipline plan at your school site. This is part of the consistency issue discussed in chapter one. At my site, the colored cards discipline with the following consequences:

> **green**: no infractions committed
>
> no consequence, no point reduction

pink: one infraction committed

　　five minute loss of recess, 10 points lost

> **yellow**: two infractions committed
>
> ten minute loss of recess, 20 points lost

red: three infractions committed

　　fifteen minute loss of recess, 30 points lost

　　call home and/or parent-teacher conference

In addition to consequences in the form of lost recess, I also inform parents via behavior reports. In chapter 14, I discuss in detail how to successfully implement the use of weekly academic/behavior reports. In short, the lost points are deducted from the 100 points that all students commence with on Monday morning. If specific behavior patterns occur repeatedly, you may want to note them in the comment section of the behavior report. Parents appreciate details, especially when their child has lost a substantial amount of points.

The loss of recess is a consequence that exacts immediate behavior modification. No student wants to lose free time with his/her friends. The loss of recess makes a significant impact and its repeated loss makes a deep impression on the student as to why the recess or a part there of, was forfeited.

> **Special Note:** Use the card system judiciously. Do not send a student to turn a card for every little thing. Make sure the infraction merits turning a card. For example: I will not have students turn a card for losing a pencil or forgetting to raise their hand every once in a while. However, if one of these behaviors persists repeatedly then a turned card may be in order. Furthermore, if students turn cards for every little thing, the impact of turning a card diminishes. They become desensitized, angered by constant recess loss and possibly desirous of additional negative attention. In my class, when a student turns a card they know that their behavior was inappropriate and merited the consequence.

The Talk During Recess

The "talk-during-recess" can happen at anytime when you can do one-on-one work with a student. I do not recommend this strategy with other students in the classroom. Their presence is too distracting. Usually when a teacher keeps a student in during recess or after school, there is some sort of discussion about why the student is not at recess or has not been dismissed for the day with all the other students. After years of watching teachers handle these "challenging" students, I have come to the conclusion that we say too much. We need to stop lecturing the student about why they are with us during recess or afterschool. They already know why! And they don't need you to tell them!

I have four questions I ask my students. These questions allow them to talk, accept responsibility for their actions, understand the consequences and hopefully change poor behavior patterns. The following are those questions:

1. **What happened?**
2. **Why are we concerned?**
3. **What could you have done differently that would be better for you?**
4. **What consequence would be fair and build responsibility for your future actions?**

Are these questions a cure-all? Absolutely not! However, they lay a firm foundation for better behavior. Try them, you may be surprised.

Rewards

My most powerful reward is praise. We are no different than children. We, too, appreciate an acknowledgment of our efforts. My most effective medium of praise is the *weekly academic/behavior report*. It goes home every Monday. On it is a short synopsis of the student's academic progress and citizenship/behavior in the classroom. My students strive for one hundred points. They know that a positive and complimentary report with one hundred points will equate to additional recognition from parents, possibly a reward (which may come in many forms: trip to the park, ball game, new toy, etc.) and especially pride in themselves for a job well done. I discuss the *weekly acdemic/behavior report* in detail in chapter 14.

Additionally, every Friday, I have a raffle from which no one is excluded. I have everyone's name on a ticket in a can. I choose four names. Those chosen receive a small prize, usually a food item. I also give a similar prize for all those that received 100% on the spelling quiz. These two activities take place on Friday, during the last ten minutes of class. My students love the raffle. Yes, they want the prize, but more than food, they are desirous of having their name pulled and called; recognition and validation of their existence.

CHAPTER 7
CLASSROOM HELPERS

In the last chapter, I mentioned the importance of teaching responsibility, building teamwork and creating community in the classroom. The following are my classroom helpers and their specific duties.

General Guidelines For All Helpers

All classroom helper positions are changed on a weekly basis. I know that some teachers change duties on a daily basis. However, I feel weekly assignments create more continuity and deeper understanding about one's role as the teacher's helper. Five days imprints and reinforces much deeper than one does. All positions are rotated throughout the course of the school year. I never exclude anyone based on behavior or academic performance. Everyone participates.

All classroom helpers' names are posted in a place that is clearly visible to all members of the class. I use a laminated sheet with lines that has each helper written out and then put post-its, with student names, next to the helper name. This way each week, all I have to do is pull the post-its off and put new ones up. I even use the same set of post-its, with student names for months. Usually, I replace them when they no longer will stick to my laminated sheet. This system is quick, convenient and efficient.

Line Leader

This helper is the first in line. He/she will start my line for recess, library hour, PE, lunch, assemblies, etc. I find this helper extremely useful for several reasons. First, when my class hears me call line leader and sees the student open the door to line up in the hall, they start getting ready to go and need less prompting. I say, "line leader" and they get quiet, stop squirming (or squirm less) in their seats, get appropriate items ready to go (jacket, ball, snack, etc.) and prepare themselves to be released by tables.

Second, the line leader can halt the line, resume its course, lead it to the desired destination, etc. much quicker than a non-line leader helper. They know they are in charge and much more attentive to the teacher. They understand they are responsible for the line and play a key role in getting from one place to another. Lastly, this helper reduces the running syndrome. A line leader sets the pace. Your line will never be perfect. However, with a line leader many problems are reduced or eliminated.

> **Line Leader Duties:**
>
> 1. First in line for all class movement as a whole.
>
> 2. Regulates the speed and straightness of the line.
>
> 3. Is attentive to teacher's commands: stop, go, take a right/left, etc.
>
> 4. Knows destinations of class and leads them. The class will follow and not get lost.
>
> 5. Opens appropriate door or doors for fluid class ingress or egress from classroom.
>
> 6. Sets the general tone of the line.

Library Helper

Every week, my class goes to the school library. They are able to check-out a book. They keep the book for a week and then must return it if they want to get another. My librarian prefers to get all the books the day before and in one big pile. It is quicker and more convenient to check them back in and reshelve them. The librarian helper or helpers, depending on how many books are returned, carries the books to the library. At my school, this activity occurs once a week.

> ### Library Helper Duties
>
> 1. Gathers all books from designated area or entire class when instructed by teacher.
>
> 2. When all books have been collected and the librarian helper knows who forgot their book, he/she then informs the teacher with one complete list. Put that list on the blackboard, visible to all students. This reminds those who forgot their book and it gives you quick access to remind students at the end of the day.
>
> 3. Delivers all books from the class to the library.
>
> 4. Brings any and all updates from the library back to the teacher. This could include canceled time, modified or new library hours, and missing books notices for your class, etc.

Office Helper

The office helper is your principal delivery student. They take attendance and notices to the main office, drop-off homework, supplies, etc. to other classrooms, deliver messages throughout the school, or any other basic "gopher" duty. When you send your office helper on an assignment that is out of the normal routine, give them good instructions about where to go, what to do and whom to talk to. I have had teachers send me students that had absolutely no clue what they were doing, where they were going or with whom they needed to talk. This is a great helper position for building organization and interpersonal communication skills. I usually give my helpers verbal instructions and a written note to be delivered. This way if the receiver of the message has a question, my helper will most likely have an accurate and complete answer.

Office Helper Duties

1. Delivers any and all documents and messages to different destinations within the school.

2. Brings back any and all documents and messages to the teacher or teacher's aide

3. Is familiar with the school: main office, counselor's office, nurse's office, classrooms, cafeteria and auditorium.

4. Understands the assignment, and can respond with follow-up information if necessary.

Pencil Sharpener

In my classroom, pencils are a valuable commodity. Without them the learning process ceases. I have tried several systems in regard to keeping a pencil in all my students' hands. If they keep them indefinitely, I find that pencils are sharpened to death quicker, lost, stolen, misplaced, or just disappear. In my class, the teacher keeps all pencils, hands them out when needed and collects them when finished. I also keep a ready supply of extras with sharpened points. Students know that they can get up, exchange the broken one for another sharpened one. All pencils are kept in a box lid from photocopy paper. It is labeled **PENCILS**. It is always kept in the same place.

> **Special note:** Pencil sharpening is very disruptive during lessons. I keep an electric sharpener in the closet, bring it out at the end of the day, sharpen all my pencils for the following day and then put it away again. Some students thrive on pencil sharpening as a means to get out of their seats, to move around, to get attention and to disrupt the class. This is where the Pencil Sharpener Helper becomes essential. At the end of the day, after all pencils have been collected, the Pencil Sharpener Helper will sharpen all pencils.

Pencil Sharpener Duties

1. During last five minutes of the school day, he/she gets electric sharpener, all pencils from pencil box, sharpens them and returns them to the pencil box.

2. Empties pencil shavings and returns electric sharpener to assigned area.

3. Informs teacher if supply of pencils is depleted or just running low. The teacher can then replenish the supply.

Trash Helper

In my classroom, there are four trash cans strategically placed. At the end of the day, the custodians empty the trash. Their time is limited in each classroom. I attempt to make their trash collection as quick as possible by having all my trash cans by the door. They open the door, reach inside, grab all four and then put them all back. It is quicker and easier than walking all over the room. They greatly appreciate it. Work with your custodians and they will work with you. During the last five minutes of class, my Trash Helper ensures that all four cans are placed at the door. Additionally, they will return them to their assigned areas the following morning.

Trash Helper Duties

1. Ensures that all trash cans in the classroom are placed together in a preassigned area convenient for the custodians.

Card Arranger

In prior chapters, I explained my attendance system with cards. After I have taken attendance, my card arranger will then turn-over all the cards with the names showing. Throughout the course of the day, I need to refer to names and numbers. This gives me a ready resource. I usually have the Card Arranger turn cards within half an hour of taking attendance.

Card Arranger Duties

1. Ensures all cards are turned over and present in the attendance name holder on the wall.

2. Informs the teacher if any cards are missing or need to be replaced.

Flag Monitor

Every day my class commences with the Pledge of Allegiance and the National Anthem. One student is responsible for getting the class started with the Pledge. They say, "right hand over your heart" and make sure all are doing it, and then say, "ready begin." The class will then recite the Pledge of Allegiance.

Flag Monitor Duties

1. They confirm that all are standing, have their right hand over their heart and are looking at the flag.

2. They start the Pledge with "ready begin."

Music Monitor

Directly after the Pledge of Allegiance, my students sing the National Anthem. I have one student, standing at the ready, by the record player. As soon as the pledge is finished, the Music Monitor turns on the *Star Spangled Banner* and the students commence singing. He/she will also turn off the record player once the song is over.

Music Monitor Duties

1. Be at the ready to turn on the National Anthem directly prior to saying the Pledge.

2. Turn the record player on and off at the teacher's prompt (nod of the head).

> **Special note:** The National Anthem is sung at many places in the Unites States (ball games, military functions, on the TV, in schools, parades, etc.). Make the National Anthem the song you sing in your class. They will take it with them for the rest of their lives. More than half of my class, within the first four months of school, told me that they heard the song somewhere else outside of school. Furthermore, they sang along. Parents have also commented how proud they were that their son or daughter knew the "Star Spangled Banner". Do not let the high keys of the song scare you. Your students will do just fine. There are also versions recorded in lower keys. I currently use one recorded in A flat.

Door and Light Helper

Throughout the course of the day, my doors open and close depending on noise in the hall, temperature of the room, amount of activity/noise my lesson produces, etc. I prefer not to interrupt my lesson to open and close it. Furthermore, there are times when my lights are turned on and off. These two functions in my classroom are easily handled by one helper. When I need the door opened/closed or lights on/off, I will announce to my Door/Light Helper, "lights, please" or "door, please". They perform the duty, I continue the lesson and the disruption factor is minimal.

> **Door and Light Helper Duties**
>
> 1. Opens/closes door when instructed.
>
> 2. Turns lights on/off when instructed.
>
> 3. Performs duties quickly with minimal disruption and returns to seat and resumes work.

Table Captains

Of all my helpers, the Table Captains are the most important. They are called upon many times throughout the day to do a variety of activities. First, I must digress a little about how my desks are arranged. As shown in the photograph below, I prefer a more traditional classroom desk arrangement. The use of Table Captains will work with almost every arrangement, but I feel that this set-up is the most effective with Table Captains. Rows allow all students to face the front of the class. If I need to tell them something or respond to a question, we, as a class, make contact quicker and more effectively. Basically all eyes are forward and attentive. With a set-up such as this, my Table Captains can respond quicker to my directions. Please refer to chapter 10 for more information about desk arrangements. They facilitate varied teaching methodologies such as direct instruction, cooperative learning groups and kinesthetic activities.

Table Captains are responsible for distributing and collecting a variety of items from their respective tables. They are very busy throughout the course of the day. Let me give you a few examples of their duties. In the morning, I collect homework, permission slips, academic/behavior reports, journals, etc. My Table Captains collect these items from all the students at their table and bring them to me.

Captains are assigned for the entire week. I rotate them down the row as the weeks progress. Everyone is a Table Captain. No one is excluded. Of all my helpers, the Table Captain's position is the most important for building a sense of responsibility. A whole table, four to six other students, count on the Captain to get them the supplies needed to accomplish lessons and assignments. They also learn a great deal about organization. While handing out or collecting items, they quickly learn that being organized is essential for accomplishing the task at hand.

Lastly, and most importantly, the Captain and students at the respective table learn to work as a team. If the students do not cooperate with the Captain, the entire process is more cumbersome. I find that elementary students love to work together. There will always be little problems or complaints, but nothing that a quick word or two can not fix. As the weeks progress and the rotating continues, the students get very good at being Table Captain.

I find that positioning myself at the front of the class and using key words is the best procedure for getting Captains' attention. In Chapter 6, I will discuss my philosophy about communication and explain in detail why the following procedure is important. Once I have the Captains' attention, I tell them in a **succinct** sentence(s) what they must accomplish. Here is an example. I want to collect the homework.

My Captains know that I collect homework in a specific order and separately. I will announce, **"Captains, I need the math homework and a list of who did not do it, please."** I say nothing more. They know that I need all the math homework from their table and also a list of who did not do it. They bring it to me, tell me who did not do it by name and number, and I record it on my clipboard. Then I make another announcement, **"Captains, I need the Language Arts homework and a list of who did not do it."** They bring it to me, tell me who does not have one by name and number, and I record it on my clipboard. Then I announce, **"Captains, I need all permission slips and who does not have them."** They bring it to me, tell me who does not have it by name and number, and I record it on my clipboard.

This is one example of a systematic and well-defined routine. My students understand exactly what needs to be accomplished and how to do it. You can hand-out or collect pencils, journals, books, paper, crayons, scissors, etc. If you attempted to do this yourself, you would waste much time throughout the course of the day and exhaust yourself. Assign Captains and use them. They are your most important helpers.

Table Captain Duties

1. **Distribute supplies that need to be handed-out to the entire class or to individual students and collect supplies upon completion of the activity.**

2. **Inform you about who did not do homework, forgot to bring permission slips, behavior reports or any other item that requires accountability.**

3. **To be attentive and responsive to all direction from the teacher and aide.**

Concluding Words About Helpers

Your classroom helpers are an integral part of your classroom structure. They maximize time-on-task and expedite accomplishment of lessons and assignments. The more you use them, the more responsibility they learn and the more efficiently your class will run. You are one (1) teacher with many students. You can not do it all alone! Your students are eager to help you. Allow them the opportunity to assist and to be a part of managing the class. In the next chapter, effective and dynamic communication techniques will enhance your ability to teach students and manage your classroom.

Notes . .

CHAPTER 8

HOW TO COMMUNICATE EFFECTIVELY: SAYING MORE BY SAYING LESS

Several years ago, I went to a workshop on classroom management. The presenter had been a teacher in my district for more than ten years. One of his principal premises about classroom management was that teachers talk too much. Their message was unclear and cluttered with unnecessary words and sentences. He contextualized this point by asking if anyone had ever been to a meeting and tuned-out after the first thirty minutes. We all said, "yes." He then proceeded to ask us "why." Within five minutes, the group agreed that most presenters at workshops, meetings, symposiums, classes, conferences, etc. do not present material clearly or succinctly. They add extraneous information and give verbose explanations. This is one of the primary reasons why speakers lose their audience. It is no different with children. If you go on forever, they will tune-out and not listen. His point was cogent and the solution was simple; say more by saying less. During his presentation, he gave us many ideas. The three that impressed me the most were the use of hand signals, diverse attention getting sounds and succinct and well defined statements.

I found hand signals to be a revolutionary concept in reducing frequent and repetitive requests that traditionally pulled students off-task and disrupted classroom decorum. Two requests in my classroom occur very frequently: bathroom and water. My first year, I was almost driven to the point of insanity with students asking to go to the bathroom or getting a drink of water. It was very disruptive to be in the middle of a lesson and have a student raise his/her hand or call out, "Mr. Remy, may I go to the bathroom?" or "May I get a drink of water?" This not only disrupted the class, but set in motion a chain reaction. All of sudden five or six students now wanted to go to the bathroom. This was more disruption than was tolerable or acceptable.

The solution was simple. When a student wanted to go to drink water he/she raised his/her hand with his/her index finger extended and the others curled. This signaled me that they wanted to drink water. I would then nod yes or no. No words were exchanged, the disruption was minimized, many other students never even took notice, and the student quietly got up, drank water, returned to his/her seat and resumed work.

This also held true with going to the bathroom. Students would raise their hand with two fingers extended (those used to make a peace sign) and the rest curled. This signaled a desire to go to the bathroom. I would either nod yes or no and the same effects would be experienced as those during asking permission for water. For two years, I have used this system. The students learn very quickly, respect the system and have seldom abused it.

> **Special note: if a student should ask permission for water or the bathroom incorrectly, ask them, "How do we ask permission for water/bathroom?" Almost always they will say with a hand raised and finger(s) extended. Have them return to their seat (if not seated) and do it correctly, before you allow them to drink water or go to the bathroom. Once done correctly, reinforce the system through practice, modeling and praise.**

Another idea, I found to be fascinating was the use of diverse sounds for getting student attention, preparing for another activity or making an announcement. This presenter used about fifteen different sounds in his classroom for everything from stop, look, listen (eyes-to-the-front) to acknowledging a great response to a question. I have never been able to incorporate that many sounds into my routine. However, for a while, I used a small sound maker to get everyone's attention. When heard, students would stop, look at the teacher, raise their hand and stop talking. I would then make my announcement, commence teaching or shift to another activity. The system worked well. The only draw back was that my sound maker was not loud enough. At times, some students did not hear it. From using this system, my own technique evolved.

When I needed the attention of the class for one of many reasons, I would announce, **"eyes on me"** and raise my hand. In most cases, the class would stop, look and listen. Sometimes, I found that a second or third announcement was necessary or the class needed an extra minute or so depending on their activity. At this point, many teachers would start talking too much. I say, **"eyes on me"** a second, maybe a third time. At this point, I will say, **"eyes on me and show me when you're ready."** I then stand in front of the class, silently, hand raised and waiting. I can not remember the last time that this technique did not work. Usually my elementary students get each other to quiet down. It is a chain reaction that results in stop, look, listen within 15-20 seconds or less.

These are the first two basic ways to reduce the amount of unnecessary chatter in a classroom. The third is the use of concise, lucid sentences. I limit spoken words by having key words for Classroom Helpers. In the prior chapter, Classroom Helper duties were explicated in detail. The same key words are employed to acquire the desired activity from the Classroom Helper. I feel it is so important that I will review them by specific Classroom Helper and activity.

Line Leader

"Line Leader, please": They know to open the door and be in the hall.

"Left, right, stop, go, or wait here please."

"Line Leader, auditorium please."(or specified destination)

Library Helper

"Library Helper, collect books please": They know to grab already collected books or books from specific students and take them to the library.

Office Runner

"Office runner, to the office please" (or specified destination)

Pencil Sharpener

"Pencil Helper, pencils please": They know to get the pencils from the box, sharpen them, return them to the box and empty shavings from the electric pencil sharpener.

Trash Helper

"Trash Helper, trash cans please": They know to bring all my cans to the specified spot by the door.

Card Arranger

"Card Helper, cards please": They know to turn-over all the cards and ensure they are in order and all present.

Flag Monitor

"Flag Monitor": They know to say, "right hand over your heart," look around, make sure everyone has their hand over their heart, is silent and ready to pledge allegiance. They follow with "ready begin." The class pledges.

Music Monitor

The Music Monitor is looking at me. I nod, and they turn on the record player, tape player or CD player. The class sings the National Anthem.

Door and Lights Helper

"Door, please": They open or close the door. The opposite of what it was.
"Lights, please": They turn the lights on or off. The opposite of what it was.

Table Captains

Commands vary with this helper. Always try to limit the amount of words. Here are a few key examples.

"Captains please": They know to come to the front of the class and are prepared to distribute materials.

"Captains, math homework please"(or other specified item to collect:

Language Arts homework, permission slips, library books, etc.): They know to collect this item from their entire table and bring it to the teacher.

"Captains, books, please": They know to get books from the shelf and give one to each person at their table.

> **As you develop succinct and precise statements of your own, write them in the area below and on the following page.**

Notes . .

CHAPTER 9
HOMEWORK COLLECTION

Most school districts require that homework is assigned every night. However, some teachers modify this regulation and assign it only several nights a week or only Monday through Thursday allowing a break during the weekend. I recommend assigning it every day, Monday through Friday. I believe the more reinforcement outside the class, the more progress made in class. My class is assigned math and language arts homework. I have thirty (30) students, therefore, I collect approximately sixty (60) pieces of homework per day. That is a lot of paper! The system I am about to explain will enable you to collect it, check who did it and record it in a matter of a few minutes.

Collection of Homework

Do not waste valuable instruction time. Collect all your homework via Table Captains. They will collect the homework in an organized manner, inform you about who did not do it and give you that person's number. Some mornings, I find myself collecting a mountain of paperwork. This may include two sets of homework (math and language arts), permission slips, conference confirmations, behavior reports, notifications requiring signatures, Federal Survey cards, etc. An average morning at my school site sees the collection of about ninety (90) to one hundred and twenty (120) pieces of paper. The following are recommendations for collecting this paper work and keeping it organized.

Recommendations

1. Table Captains bring one set of homework or paper work up to the teacher at a time. Do not accept anything else, only that which you requested. If you get a variety of items from the Table Captains, recording, organizing and collection in general becomes chaotic. For example, "Table Captains, math homework, please." Your Table Captains will bring you all the math homework and **ONLY** the math homework.

2. Record who did not do homework by number. Train the Captains to go to a designated spot. When they arrive, they hand you the homework and tell you what number did not do it. That is all you need to know. In certain cases, a student may need to give an explanation. Keep it short and get back to that student a little later when the commotion level is lower. In the next section, I will explain the homework number sheet.

3. The amount of paper work received will dictate the space required to keep it organized. Ensure that you have plenty of space. I usually use my desk and a long window sill/counter space. Both are within close proximity to each other. As I receive the homework and/or paperwork I keep it in neat organized piles. Each pile is only one item. Do not mix the items. If you have to search for items in disorganized piles, you will waste inordinate amounts of time and experience frustration. **MY RULE OF THUMB: KEEP IT ORGANIZED!**

4. If one of your Table Captains brings the wrong item or jumps the gun with something you have not requested, tell them to take it back to their desk and wait. It is very important to train them properly. This exercise is more than just collecting

paper work. It is an exercise in listening and following directions. The first couple of days will be a little rough; however, after that your students will amaze you and even enjoy the responsibility.

Checking Who Did Not Do The Homework

There will always be those who do not complete the homework for one reason or another. You must find out who that person(s) is and make them responsible for their choice.

Special Note: All those that choose not to do their homework, stay in at recess, lunch recess and after school (if necessary) to complete it. Losing recess for several days or several times over the weeks reinforces homework completion. To an elementary student, the loss of recess is significant. They want to be outside with their friends, not inside doing homework from the night before. <u>Please check with your district office prior to implementing this intervention. There might be regulations prohibiting it.</u>

Recording Homework Completion

As stated previously, all students have a number. Your Table Captains inform you via student numbers who did not complete the homework. At this point, what is needed is a device to quickly and efficiently record homework completion.

I use a form with everyone's number. If a student has not completed the homework, I circle his/her number. This takes less than a second and gives me a quick reference so I know who is staying in at recess to do their work. The following is an example of how the form is arranged. On page 73 is a black-line master you can photocopy for use in your class.

Assignment: <u>Three Times Each Quiz</u> Date: <u>05/21/97</u>

① 2   3   4   5   ⑥   7   8   9   ⑩   11 12 13 14
15 16 17 18 19 20 21 22 23 24 25 26
27 28 29 30 31 32 33 34 35 36 37 38

For example numbers 1, 6 and 10 did not complete their homework.

Assignment: <u>Dictionary Drill</u> Date: <u>05/22/97</u>   (Complete)

1   2   3   4   5   6   7   8   9   10 11 12 13 14
15 16 17 18 19 20 21 22 23 24 25 26
27 28 29 30 31 32 33 34 35 36 37 38

The May 22nd example demonstrates a day when all students completed the homework assignment. If all students successfully completed the homework, I write in parenthesis "**COMPLETE.**" This method reminds me that I checked all the homework and no numbers needed to be circled, i.e., all students did the homework.

Page # _____

Homework Assignment Sheet Class _____ Grade _____

Assignment:_____ Date:_____

1 2 3 4 5 6 7 8 9 10 11 12 13 14
15 16 17 18 19 20 21 22 23 24 25 26
27 28 29 30 31 32 33 34 35 36 37 38

Assignment:_____ Date:_____

1 2 3 4 5 6 7 8 9 10 11 12 13 14
15 16 17 18 19 20 21 22 23 24 25 26
27 28 29 30 31 32 33 34 35 36 37 38

Assignment:_____ Date:_____

1 2 3 4 5 6 7 8 9 10 11 12 13 14
15 16 17 18 19 20 21 22 23 24 25 26
27 28 29 30 31 32 33 34 35 36 37 38

Assignment:_____ Date:_____

1 2 3 4 5 6 7 8 9 10 11 12 13 14
15 16 17 18 19 20 21 22 23 24 25 26
27 28 29 30 31 32 33 34 35 36 37 38

Assignment:_____ Date:_____

1 2 3 4 5 6 7 8 9 10 11 12 13 14
15 16 17 18 19 20 21 22 23 24 25 26
27 28 29 30 31 32 33 34 35 36 37 38

Notes . .

CHAPTER 10
DESK ARRANGEMENT

Over the past three years, I have tried several different table or seating arrangements in my classroom. My preferred arrangement is rows. I find the arrangement works best with my system of Table Captains, size of my classroom, type of desks supplied by the school and student population. Your desk arrangement is very personal and dependent on several different variables. The first arrangement shown below is my preferred, the others have been used and work fairly well.

X = One (1) Desk

Desks in Rows

Front-of-Class

X	X	X	X	X	X
X	X	X	X	X	X
X	X	X	X	X	X
X	X	X	X	X	X
X	X	X	X	X	X
X	X	X	X	X	X

As stated earlier, this is my preferred desk arrangement. I find that students are able to pay attention to me when needed with greater focus. There is less distraction from neighbors, decreased chatter and increased time-on-task. They are also **ALL** facing toward the same direction. No one needs to turn around to pay attention: only look up and listen. Elementary students squirm at times. Space is one of several elements that reduces the squirm factor. If one student squirms, it can become a chain reaction.

Desks in Groups

Front-of-Class

```
  X X                           X X
  X X                           X X
  X X                           X X
                X X
                X X
                X X

  X X                           X X
  X X                           X X
  X X                           X X
```

For an entire school year, I employed this desk arrangement. I did not find it to be that effective. When students faced each other chatter increased, focus on the teacher decreased or happened much slower and at times cheating occurred. I did prefer this arrangement when I taught science or conducted kinesthetic/hands-on projects. We did a great deal of group work during experiments. This arrangement allowed for more desk space. Experiments almost always necessitate using equipment that must be set-up. A single desk does not provide adequate room.

Desks in a "U" Shape

Front-of-Class

```
X                                                    X
X X                                                X X
X                                                    X
X X                                                X X
X                                                    X
X X                                                X X
X                                                    X
X X                                                X X
X                                                    X
 X X X X X X X X X X X X X X X X X X
```

The "U" shape desk arrangement allows a teacher the opportunity to have all students facing forward. There is also a fair degree of space between students; not quite as much as rows, but better than desks in groups. This set-up also gives a teacher more consolidated desk top space for group projects, experiments, art work, etc. The greatest limitation is impeded student avenues of movement. Students are not able to move from one area to another with the same degree of fluidity as with desks in a row or desks in groups.

There are many different variations of the following desk arrangements. I used the three depicted over the last three (3) years. They are time and student tested. My preferred arrangement is rows. However, every teacher requires or prefers desks in a certain arrangement. My advice is that you try the preceding three patterns, get a feel for them, and then decide what is best for you. You may also want to modify a pattern due to classroom size and structure, student population, desks supplied and/or lessons taught.

Notes . .

CHAPTER 11
START THE DAY PATRIOTICALLY

The Pledge of Allegiance and singing a patriotic song is usually mandated or highly recommended by school districts across the United States. I have worked at two different sites and done about a dozen observations at others. I can not remember a classroom that did not start the day without the pledge and a song. It is usually one of the first items on a teacher's agenda in the morning. Commencing the day with the pledge and a song is important for several reasons, some of which are not as obvious as others. The following paragraph will expand on importance and composition of starting the day patriotically.

Please, remember to use your Flag Monitor and Music Monitor for this activity. For convenience, I previously included their duties on pages 51 & 52 in chapter seven.

Flag Monitor

Every day my class commences with the Pledge of Allegiance and National Anthem. One student is responsible for getting the class started with the pledge. They say, "right hand over your heart" and make sure all are doing it, and then say, "ready begin." The class will then recite the Pledge of Allegiance.

Flag Monitor Duties

1. **They confirm that all are standing, have their right hand over their heart and are looking at the flag.**

2. **They start the pledge with "ready begin."**

Music Monitor

Directly after the Pledge of Allegiance, my students sing the National Anthem. I have one student, standing at the ready, by the record player. As soon as the pledge is finished, the Music Monitor turns on the *Star Spangled Banner* and the students commence singing. He/she will also turn off the record player once the song is over.

Music Monitor Duties

1. Be at the ready to turn on the National Anthem directly prior to saying the Pledge.

2. Turn on the record player at the teacher's prompt (nod of the head) and turn it off.

The National Anthem: "Star Spangled Banner"

I have a general rule of thumb in regards to lessons. I attempt to make every lesson taught have a practical application. My class sings the *Star Spangled Banner* by Francis Scott Key. We sing this song because it is the National Anthem of the United States. It is recognized nationally and internationally. It is sung in many places: military functions, ball games, parades, special or honorary functions, etc. We sing a song that they will sing for the rest of their lives.

During the first three months of singing the song, I had several students tell me that they sang the song at ball games, along with the television or at some special function. They related this activity with pride and excitement.

They impressed the adults around them, their parents and even themselves. Several parents, during Parent-Teacher Conferences, even commented that their child had sung the National Anthem. This aspect of the song connects and reinforces my students' understanding about the importance of a nation's patriotic song. It also promotes an understanding of living in a country and belonging. The more integrated they feel, the better they will interact in American society. This is only one small piece of the puzzle that makes a child a successful adult, but it is an important one.

The *Star Spangled Banner* comes in several different keys. I have a version in A flat. It is easier for the students, and myself, to sing. Do not be scared-off by the fact that the song has a high range of notes. Your students will impress you with their ability to sing the song and sing it well. It took my class about two weeks to get the song down and memorize the words.

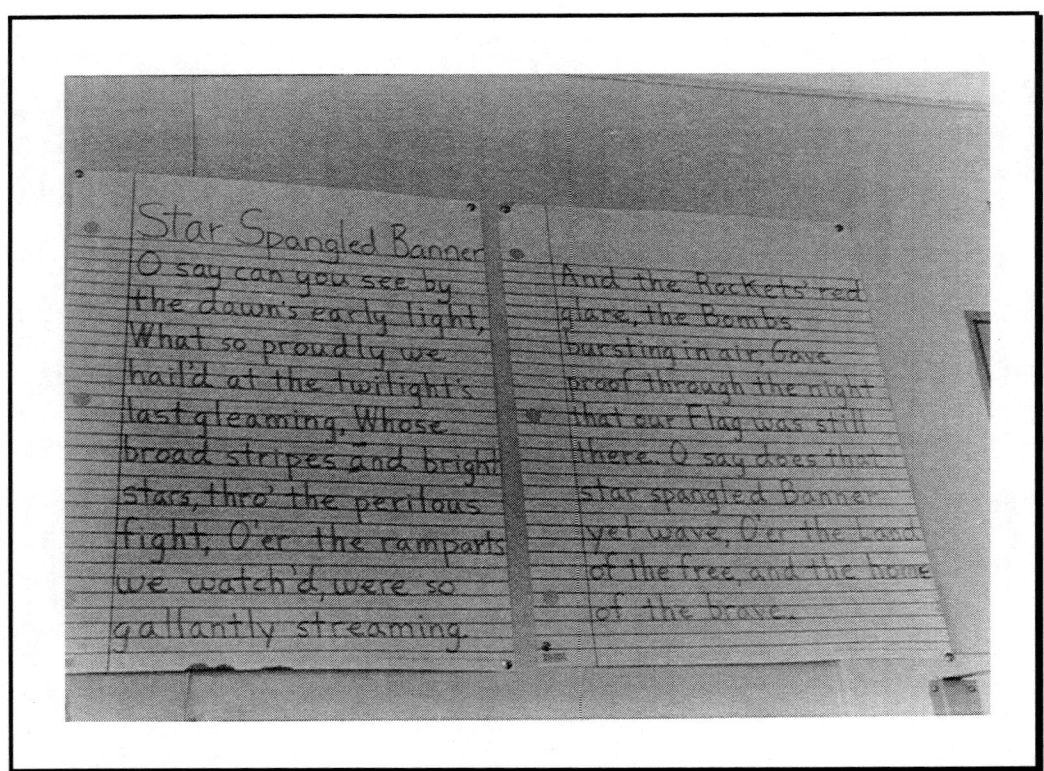

Just to the side of the American flag, I have posted the words to the National Anthem. They are in clear view and easily read by the entire class. With the words posted, the students sing with greater fluency and memorize with more retention.

If possible, get some literature on why Francis Scott Key wrote the *Star Spangled Banner*. There is plenty of information on the War of 1812 and the Battle of Baltimore. If your students understand Key's inspiration for writing the poem that was later transformed into our National Anthem, they will sing with more enthusiasm, pride and patriotism for their country. I found a picture book about Francis Scott Key's life and focused on the events leading to the writing of the *Star Spangled Banner*. My students still repeat facts about the Battle of Baltimore, bombs bursting in the air, the British ships and Fort McHenry. Additionally, explain that the thirteen stripes represent the original thirteen colonies and each of the fifty stars a state in the Union.

Notes . .

CHAPTER 12
OPENING ACTIVITIES: CALENDAR, ONES-TENS-HUNDREDS AND WEATHER

In my class, the students know that once the pledge and the *Star Spangled Banner* are completed, it is time to get serious and down to work. Opening activities are designed to get the students ready for a day of learning. I start with calendar activities. It allows my students the opportunity to settle down gradually and get ready for the day's lessons. Some school districts require a public speaking and/or visual and performing arts component. In most cases this will fulfill the requirement. It also teaches the concepts of time (months, days, years and seasons), mathematics (ones-tens-hundreds) and weather conditions (sunny, rainy, foggy, overcast, hot, cold, etc.). The following sections will walk you through the process.

> **Special Note: I do the calendar activities everyday. I feel it is important, not only to have a routine, but also to convey an understanding about the passage of time. Stress how quickly it passes and that everyday needs to be productive.**
>
> **Tell them that everyday must count!**

The List

Every student participates in the morning activities. I have a roster hanging on a clip board by the calendar activities area in my room. Each day, three students participate in the activities. It takes approximately ten (10) school days to have the whole class participate. I start at the top-of-the-list and work my way to the bottom. I go in order and do not jump around. When I reach the bottom, I start at the top again. I usually put a little line next to the name and then the second time around I make the line an "X" by crossing it. This system will keep you from skipping a student. This activity is intended for kindergarten through third grade and second language learners in a sheltered language environment up to the fifth grade.

The Calendar

The calendar is broken into two parts. Two students will do these parts.

Student One (1)

You call their name off the roster. They come to the front of the class.

1. They will move the circle from yesterday's number date on the calendar itself to the current day.

Please move the circle to today's date.

They will then turn, face the class and in a clear and loud voice say the date. For example: Today is December sixth, 1996. Only accept a full sentence.

2. At this point you will have the entire class repeat in choral response the date in the same way as student one.

Everyone, together; what is today's date?

3. Then the student is asked if anyone has a birthday today.

Do we have a birthday today?

They will then answer yes or no. If yes, **who and how old**; if no, **when is the next birthday and whose.** Student one has now completed his/her part of the calendar activity.

Special Note: You will ask the class or check your roster for birthdays. At the end of each month ask for the succeeding month's birthdays and keep track of them on a birthday roster in your calendar area.

Student Two (2)

As soon as student one sits down, call up the next person on your roster. He/she is student two. This student will help you with counting. He/she gets a straw from your pencil box with calendar supplies and places it in the ones, tens or hundreds, depending on how many days have passed. For example, if it were the 112th day of school you would have one bundle of one hundred straws in the hundreds' cup, one bundle of ten straws in the tens' cup and two single straws in the ones' cup. Student two places the straw in the appropriate cup and then informs the class how many days have passed.

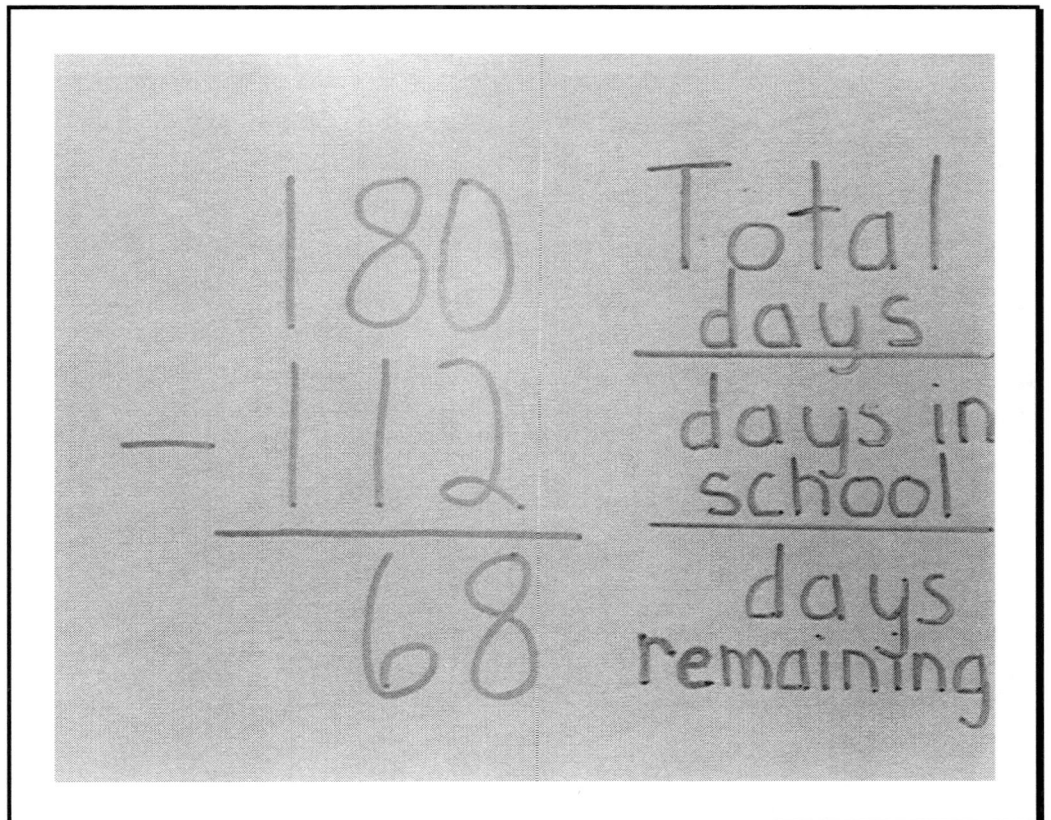

1. **How many straws are in the hundreds' cup?**

They reply, "There are one-hundred straws in the hundreds' cup."

2. **How many straws are in the tens' cup?**

They reply, "There are ten straws in the tens' cup."

3. **How many straws are in the ones' cup?**

They reply, "There are two straws in the ones' cup."

4. **How many total straws?**

They reply, "There are one-hundred and twelve straws."

5. **How many days in school?**

They reply, "We have been in school for one-hundred and twelve days."

At this point they will put a tally mark on the sheet labeled Tally Sheet. This keeps track of the days in school and also teaches groups of five.

On the blackboard, you will keep track of the following information:

180 Total Days in School
- 112 Days in School
68 Days Remaining

Ask student two to tell you the following:

6. **How many total days in school this year?**
    They reply, "There are 180 total days in school."

7. **How many days in school?**
    They reply, "There are 112 days in school."

8. **How many days remaining?**
    They reply, "There are 68 days remaining."

The student does this facing the class and answering in a clear and loud voice. They may look back at the blackboard to get information; however, when responding they must face the class.

Student Three (3)

Student three does the weather. You call his/her name off the roster as you did student one and two. They all come to the front of the class. They look out of the window to get the weather report.

1. **What is the weather report for today?**
    They reply, "Today is sunny and hot."

They will tell the class what they saw. For example: "Today is cloudy and cold." "Today is sunny and hot." "Today is overcast and cold." At this point, student three will get a weather card from the pencil supply box and put it on the calendar. Then they put tally marks on the weather report sheet under the appropriate categories.

After student three has completed his/her duties, I do a brief-back. A "brief-back" is a question and answer session to confirm that all were listening and understood. I ask the following questions and then select students who have raised their hands as well as those who have not raised their hand. This is a personal judgment call. Some students participate more freely than others. If you call-on students randomly, focus on-the-lesson factor increases exponentially. If you never know when you'll be called on, you pay more attention and remain prepared at all times.

1. What is today's date?

2. What is the name of the current month?

3. What is the name of the next month?

4. What day of the week is it today? (Monday, etc.)

5. Do we have a birthday today? If not when?

6. Who can tell me the total number of days we must be in school?

7. Who can tell me the total number of days we have been in school?

8. Who can tell me how many days remain?

9. What is today's weather report?

10. In which season are we ?

At this point, I have the entire class repeat in choral response all the days of the week and all the months of the year. I use the calendar itself for the days of the week and a poster with all the months of the year. I keep the class in unison by using a pointer and a steady tempo as I point down the list of days and months.

> **Special Note:** As each student finishes his/her part, thank them for their participation. If you find students in the class not participating or talking, just stop and say, "tell me when you are ready" or ask them the question just asked of students one, two and three. Remind students that each and everyone of them will be in front of the class. Respect each student's rights and be courteous. The photographs in this chapter explicate the process better than I can in words. Study them carefully. The actual calendar items are bought in a pre-packaged school calendar. Almost any school supply store will have them. They cost about $25.

Notes . .

CHAPTER 13
PARENT LETTER HOME

Parent support is crucial in the classroom. With it, your class will have fewer behavior problems, more homework delivered on a daily basis, enhanced student desire to please parents and increased parent follow through in the areas of discipline at home, prompt signing of important forms, assistance in the classroom and support for parent-teacher conferences. Without it, much of the above will not happen. You may also experience hostile parents that pull students from your class and complain to the Principal and/or Vice Principal(s). I garner parent support through several methods. The most effective is my parent letter. It is sent home the first day of school. It welcomes parents to a new school year, explains my discipline system, describes my homework requirements and assignments, sets forth my main focus for the academic year (this will depend on the class you teach; I have taught transition/sheltered classes with a heavy emphasis on ESL) and most importantly presents my open door policy.

I welcome parents in my classroom for observations, as helpers or for conferences to address concerns. They may come and observe or help-out whenever they choose. In regard to conferences, I insist on before school or after school. I explain that I am not comfortable with interruptions during lessons. I have never had a parent disagree with this stipulation. I am in contact with my parents on a regular basis. Communication is essential for mutually beneficial parent-teacher relationship. If parents know and understand what is occurring in the classroom, you will garner their support.

I have also found that while communicating with parents frankness, honesty and genuine concern is preferred. There will be times when a parent-conference will focus on bad behavior, incomplete homework, tardiness or unsatisfactory report cards. It is best to be forthright and truthful with parents: tell the whole story. They will see through you and lose respect for what you purport to do in the classroom. The truth, for better or worse, is also a sign that you care. Genuine concern for student achievement and well being is quickly perceived by parents. Most parents have had experiences with several teachers before their child arrives in your classroom. Each teacher is a measuring stick to prior teachers. I recommend that while talking about problematic matters you suggest interventions that are feasible. You can not drop a live handgrenade on a parent without suggestions on how to defuse it. I will also tell parents that we are a team and I will work with them until an intervention succeeds. Additionally, never pass-up an opportunity to make a positive comment to a parent about their son's or daughter's citizenship or academics. Do not make parent contact a time for only discussing problems!

My school has an underlying philosophy, "All children can learn." This belief shines through everything I do in my classroom. It says we will find an effective intervention, work together as a team and never give-up. In conclusion, communication will build a strong relationship between parents and teachers. The parent letter home and an open door policy are two of your best mediums. In this chapter, I include a copy of my parent letter. With minor modifications it can be used in your classroom. In the following chapter, I discuss the Weekly Academic/Behavior Report. It too, enhances communication between teacher and parents.

Room # _____   Name of School _____   Date _____

Dear Parents:

I welcome you and your child to my classroom. With much enthusiasm, I commence this academic year of studies, learning and intellectual enrichment. Your children will continue learning the basics in mathematics, language arts, reading, literature, science, social studies, English, physical education, art and music.

In addition to these academic content areas, I hope that your child will learn to respect themselves and others, to cultivate a sense of responsibility, generosity and discipline. In order to help all children grow intellectually and socially, our classroom will have the following rules:

1. **I raise my hand if I want to talk.**
2. **I am responsible for my own actions.**
3. **I always do the best I can.**
4. **I follow directions.**
5. **I work quietly in my assigned seat.**

Each day, students are evaluated in the area of classroom behavior through a system of colored cards. I respectfully request that you ask your child every day, "With which color card did you finish the day?" If it was green, please congratulate them for a day well done.   Each colored card represents the following evaluation:

GREEN: I had an excellent day. Congratulations!!
YELLOW: I did not respect one classroom rule. I lost ten points and five minutes of recess.
PINK: I did not respect two classroom rules. I lost twenty points and ten minutes of recess.
RED: I did not respect three classroom rules. I lost thirty points and recess.

I also ask for your assistance in the area of homework completion. All homework reinforces lessons taught at school. I assign homework Monday through Friday. It is your child's obligation to complete and return it the following school day. I require homework to be well done and to demonstrate an effort to do the best work possible. If for any reason, your child is unable to complete part or all of the assigned homework, please attach a short note, signed by a parent/guardian. My homework is in the same format every week.

MONDAY: A dictation from the current week's book.

TUESDAY: A wordfind with the fifteen vocabulary words and placing all fifteen words in alphabetical order.

WEDNESDAY: Assigned pages in our weekly book to be read aloud to a parent/guardian. A parent/guardian will sign their read-aloud slip which is returned the following morning.

THURSDAY: A two-sided paper with all fifteen vocabulary words to be written ten times each. This is to reinforce the words for Friday's spelling quiz.

FRIDAY: All incorrectly spelled vocabulary words from the quiz are to be written out five times. Additionally, parents are requested to check-out books from the Public Library for their children to read on Saturday and Sunday.

Every Monday your child will take a weekly behavior report home which will inform you about their work habits and behavior. You will also see total points earned for the week. 100 points is a perfect score. It is very important for you to sign the report, write comments and ensure that the report is returned to me Tuesday morning.

Many of my students this year are the same as last year. I was very pleased with their academic progress, desire to learn, superb attitude and responsible behavior. If you ever have a question or concern, my door is always open. I am free to talk before and after school. I politely request that you do not attempt to speak with me during lessons. I rarely have a moment to talk. I look forward to the new academic school year.

Sincerely,

Mark Remy
4/5 Teacher

-----------------------cut along the dotted line---

Please sign below to confirm receipt of this letter.

_____ (Parent Signature)

Notes . .

CHAPTER 14
WEEKLY ACADEMIC AND BEHAVIOR REPORTS

Weekly academic/behavior reports are another effective medium of communication with parents. It enables parents to receive a weekly formatted report on student academic progress and classroom behavior. I send it home every Monday and it reflects the prior weeks activities. Some teachers send it home on Fridays, reporting on that current week. I prefer to have the weekend available to reflect on the past week and review records.

I also have a system based on 100 points. For every homework not completed, a student loses 10 points and for every card turned on the discipline chart 10 points are lost. A student receiving 100 points behaved well all week and turned in all homework complete. My students have always been motivated to get 100 points. Many of their parents reward them based on getting a perfect score of 100 points.

If homework was not turned in or if a specific behavior occurred, I note it in the commentary section of the Weekly Academic/Behavior Report. Parents are informed why 100 points were not obtained and students are reminded why they lost points. This helps reinforce the importance of proper classroom behavior and homework.

At the bottom of the form, you will notice a place for teacher signature and parent signature. On Mondays, the behavior report is sent home via the student. Tuesday morning, it is due back with a parent signature. Monday night parents read the report, sign it and have an opportunity to write in the parent commentary section. This allows you to acquire a pulse of what parents are thinking. Once the academic/behavior report is returned, I retain it in a specific academic/behavior report file. Each student has their own separate file. This is very helpful during conferences, consultation team meetings, grade promotions and award ceremonies. I have a running record of student progress in the areas of academics and behavior.

Remember communication is very important. The comments of parents can alert you to concerns and/or approval of what is happening in your classroom. I will not even attempt to say that the Weekly Academic/Behavior Reports do not consume resources. I slaughter half a forest a year in paper, photocopying reports and I spend at least one hour every weekend completing them. To save time, there are certain parts of the Weekly Behavior Report that are done prior to photocopying several weeks worth of reports, or as I prefer, the entire year's set. The Weekly Academic/Behavior Reports consists of student's name, teacher's name and teacher's signature. This may appear to be an extensive investment in paper and time; however, I find that my class runs much smoother and with a higher degree of accountability on everyone's part. Students understand that every week their academic performance and behavior are consistently reported to their parents. Parents are fully aware of their child's progress, and the teacher secures support from students and parents as well as keeping an open channel for two-way communication. A well run classroom, with well-behaved and enthusiastic students, supportive parents and caring teachers will always promote a more effective and responsive learning environment. On the following page, you will find a blank Weekly Academic/Behavior Report, ready for classroom use. It may be reproduced for teacher use.

Student Weekly Classroom Report

Student's Name_____Teacher_____

Student's Academic Work:

___ worked well and diligently all week.
___ worked well and diligently only part of the week.
___ did minimal work all week.
___ failed to complete homework assignments.(listed below)
    _____
    _____

___ other comments: _____
_____

Student's Citizenship:

___ behaved well and respected others all week.
___ behaved well and respected others only part of the week.
___ disruptive and uncooperative with teacher and students.
    Specific Examples: _____
_____

___ talked with others too much.
___ Parent-Teacher conference required.

Weekly Attendance Summary:

____ Perfect ____ # of Absences ____ # of Daily Tardiness

Teacher Comments:

_____
_____

Parent Comments:

_____
_____

Teacher's Signature _____ Date_____

Parent's Signature _____ Date_____

◆ The New Teacher's Survival Guide © 1997 ◆

CHAPTER 15
ACQUIRING RESOURCES FOR YOUR CLASSROOM

As a teacher, you are able to acquire many resources from public and private sources. During the last ten years while in the educational profession, I have acquired many useful and necessary teaching aids either free or at a substantially discounted price. Always ask, you might be surprised by the generosity of people from whom you make requests. The following are just a few donations that I have acquired:

> **flower pots from nurseries**
>
> **class set (35) of Thomas Guide road atlas**
>
> **chopsticks**
>
> **LCD panel for my overhead projector (heavily discounted)**
>
> **calligraphy books**
>
> **Koran and related Islamic materials**
>
> **class set (35) of newspapers: once a week**
>
> **assorted prizes for classroom recognition**
>
> **cups, plates, plasticware and napkins**
>
> **Styrofoam mannequin heads for art**
>
> **MacDonald's coupons for student achievement/recognition**

My general rule of thumb is to always try. Send a carefully and clearly drafted letter on stationary with the school letter head to the department head, general manager, president or to the person that seems most qualified to make a decision regarding donations to a school. If you get a response, always send a thank you letter regardless of whether they donate or not. You never know when you may write to that person again. The second time they may have what you need and may donate. My first source for acquiring addresses and names is through the yellow pages. Call and request the address and the name of the person to contact. I have also found teacher conventions, workshops and supply stores to be a fertile source of names, addresses and phone numbers. There will, also, be times when actually stopping at a place in person is best. For example, on page 108, I listed "flower pots from a nursery." These were used for growing plants in the classroom. I went to my neighborhood nursery and asked if they had any flower pots to be discarded. They led me to a pile of plastic pots in the back and said, "Help yourself. The more you take, the less we need to cart to the dumpster."

A community is very supportive of its schools. I find it to be the rule and not the exception that people and businesses will donate. They want to help. Remember to ask and follow-up with a thank you letter. The worst that can happen is they will say "no"; most of the time they will say "yes."

Notes . .

CHAPTER 16
YOUR TEACHING AIDE

Not all school districts have adequate funding to provide teachers with a teaching aide. If you are fortunate enough to have this luxury, the following suggestions will maximize the positive impact a teaching aide can have upon your teaching activities.

Select Your Own Teaching Aide

During my first year in the Public School System, I had the misfortune of having teaching aides assigned to me. I vividly remember several. They would show-up, get a look at the class and become overwhelmed. By the time the third one left, my intuitive abilities were keen. I was able to tell within a day if the aide would last or just not show-up the following day. Additionally, I watched other teachers have similar if not equally frustrating experiences. After about the fifth teaching aide departed, I decided to find my own aide. The young lady that I found had been a camp counselor, worked with middle school students for years and had a sense of determination, perseverance and resiliency. Since that aide, all subsequent aides have been recruited by me.

My last four teaching aides have been stellar. The only reason they depart is because they have accepted contracts as teachers. If you have the option, find your own aide. Make sure he/she is someone that has experience and/or is planning on becoming a teacher. Call Teacher Credentialing Programs and ask to have an Aide Wanted sign posted. You will get a response! Then get recommendations, make telephone calls to past employers and interview with preprepared questions. Tell them, specifically, what you expect. If possible, have them come volunteer in your class for a day or two. They can get a look at the classroom environment, get a feel for the students and see if the job is for them. You, in turn, can get a look and a feel for him/her. This job is not for everyone. Every time an aide comes and goes, it disrupts your class. A good aide is a valuable asset. I could not live without one; and you should not live with a bad one or none at all.

Your Aide's Work Area

Now that you have recruited a top-notch aide, he/she will need a place to work. I can not impress upon you enough the importance of giving your aide a workplace of his/her own. Many times, your aide will do prep work, tutoring, testing, homework/test/quiz correction, art projects, etc. This work demands space, a table and a certain degree of privacy. On the next page is a picture of my aide's work station. It is in the back of the class and fairly private.

Besides finding a place, with a table and privacy, your aide will need supplies. I recommend the following items. However, your aide may require others. Ask them what they need. You can not expect a carpenter to build a house without a hammer and nails, nor your aide to accomplish varied tasks without the necessary tools.

scissors	**colored markers**	**ruler(s)**
tape	**glue (assorted)**	**paper**
pens and pencils	**yard stick**	**paint**
brushes	**binders**	**paper cutter**
straight-edge	**stapler/extra staples**	**card board**

How To Use Your Aide

Quite simply, treat your aide like a fellow teacher. Empower them with many of the activities that you conduct throughout the course of the school day. From my experience, aides prefer to be busy accomplishing challenging tasks. Do not let them stand around. They will become bored, disillusioned with the position and more likely to quit. My last four aides, the fourth currently working with me, have all come from Teacher Credentialing Programs. All four were eager to learn as much as possible so that they would be better prepared when they got their own class. Personally, I train my aides to accomplish many tasks. The following are some of those duties:

1. **Preparation of homework and subsequent correction**
2. **Correction of tests and quizzes**
3. **Changing/creating bulletin boards**
4. **Tutoring or small group instruction**
5. **Acquiring supplies from the custodians**
6. **Checking out books from district instructional media center**
7. **Supervision during recess or PE**
8. **Cleaning-up after projects**
9. **Filing and portfolio placement of student work**

CHAPTER 17
TIPS TO STAYING HEALTHY

As a teacher, you will work in a "sea of contagion." The vast majority of it results from prolonged and intensive exposure to children with a cold or the flu. I remember my first two years well. I was sick almost every six to eight weeks. I never got anything worse than a cold, but it complicated everything inside and outside of the classroom. You do not need to suffer as much as I did. Around the end of my second year, I learned a few techniques to staying healthy. Adhere to the following list and you will be healthier.

1. Get at least seven to eight hours of sleep per night. This means even if you must go to bed early. I list this first because it is the most important health tip I will give you. Go several months with only four or five hours of sleep a night and see how you feel. Let alone how susceptible you'll be to colds and the flu.

2. Throughout the course of the day, wash your hands as frequently as possible. And do not touch your face. The more you touch your face the more you spread germs near your mouth and nose; two major points of entry for sickness. In the Military, we used to do push-ups when Drill Sergeants caught us touching our faces. As my arms ached, I learned. The lesson they instilled was valuable and worth a few hundred push-ups.

3. I take vitamins. Personally, I feel they have been a decisive weapon in the battle against sickness. The correct vitamins will keep you healthier and more energetic. I suggest the following regiment on a daily basis: 1000 mg of vitamin C, a multiple vitamin and mineral with sustained release, B100 and an anti-oxidant supplement. For those times when you feel a cold or flu coming on, echinacea & goldenseal 500 mg tablets will help to fight the infection. It is

a naturally occurring antibiotic. It has worked miracles for me. **I am not a medical doctor, nor do I profess to be one. Before using the following suggested vitamins, consult a physician if you have any questions or concerns.**

4. During recess eat a piece of fruit. I recommend an apple, peach, nectarine or plum. They are not messy to eat, do not need to be peeled or cut, and can be eaten while working with students. First and foremost, fruit is a good source of vitamins, fiber and fructose (for energy). Secondly, it will give you another burst of energy until lunch. Fatigue always wears you down and thus makes you more susceptible to sickness. Too many teachers break-out snacks high in saturated fat and low in nutrition. Do not become an over-weight teacher. Remember you are what you eat.

5. Exercise on a regular basis. I know you will be wiped out after a day with the kids, but to not work-out will give you even less energy. The stronger you are the more energy you will have. I guarantee it!

6. Control your anger and balance it with a sense of humor. Students will upset you. This is a given, but do not let it happen every day or over every little thing. When I recommended B100, it was for your nervous system. It will help combat damage sustained to your nervous system from tension, stress and anger. However, if you can keep from becoming the [above], the vitamin will not have to work as hard. In my room, I have had several different banners on the wall to help keep things in perspective. "Live the challenge," "It always works out in the end" or "Let it go." They are short sentences which remind me that it is not worth getting angry. They keep me in perspective. Remember they are just kids. They are going to do certain activities which will drive you crazy. You can either laugh about it or blow your top. I prefer to laugh about it and I hope you will do the same.

7. Wear clothing and shoes which are comfortable and allow for temperature change. I live in San Diego, California. In the morning, it can be a little chilly, 50's, but by noon it can be in the 80's and by evening back to the 50's. If I come to school in a sweater (with nothing underneath), I am in trouble. I will probably sweat until I dehydrate. Come to school wearing layers of clothing. Have the option to take clothes on and off, to remain at a comfortable temperature. Too hot or too cold, can be uncomfortable and precipitate illness. Additionally, keep a jacket in your classroom for those days that you forget to wear one or the weather changes unexpectedly.

Shoes should also be comfortable. You will be on your feet the majority of the day. If your feet hurt you will be miserable. I recommend a shoe with a flexible rubber soul. Something that takes impact well. If your feet, knees or lower back hurt, you may need to check into a new work shoe.

8. Be positive. I know that some days this will be difficult. I am just as guilty as the next person of complaining or dwelling on an issue. However, limit that behavior. Try to catch yourself and change your nuero-associations. What do I mean? Smile, greet people in a friendly manner, be helpful, say please and thank you, congratulate and praise others for a job well-done. Remember, no act of kindness ever goes unrewarded. Being positive is also good for your health. It will keep stress, frustration and anger to a minimum.

Three years ago, I organized a very intricate and involved schoolwide presentation. It took three months of planning, many telephone calls and endless meetings with school administrators and presenters. As a result of much hardwork, it was a total success. The students, teachers, administration and even presenters had an exceptional learning experience. This was rewarding in itself. However, what affected me the most was the reaction of the principal and teachers. Almost all the teachers came to my room to thank me for a job well-done. The principal even put a formal memorandum in my personnel file. The point being that the overwhelmingly positive response lifted my spirits. I felt better and taught better. All because of a few words. Your attitude is everything. Be positive and upbeat, even during difficult moments. In the end, your body will be healthier and your soul happier.

9. I mentioned fruit during recess. Now I will suggest a healthy lunch. I see some teachers, on a daily basis, eating processed, prepackaged food. Please do not do this. Eat healthy, nutritious food, which will give you sustained energy. Furthermore, I strongly recommend drinking at least a quart of water throughout the school day. It will not only keep you from dehydrating, but also reduces the chances of headaches, the impact from stress and ultimately contracting colds and the flu. Remember, "You are what you eat!"

10. In conclusion, there are other health tips which I have not included. I relate the habits and routines that work well for me. Please feel free to expand or adapt. I want you to be healthy and energetic. If you are, you will be a more effective teacher.

Notes . .

CHAPTER 18
STUDENT BEHAVIOR: MY TEN BEST TIPS

Citizenship, behavior, discipline, classroom management, interventions, social interaction, etc. are an integral part of teaching and being a teacher. I consider myself a very tough and demanding teacher. My earliest memories in grade school were of teachers that were organized, demanded high standards and refused to accept bad behavior. I remember my first grade teacher. She must have been a Drill Sergeant in another life (or maybe that one). She always demanded high standards in academics and citizenship (behavior). Students understood the importance of doing their best and never settling for anything less. It is my primary belief that without high standards your students will never realize their full potential. With this statement, as a foundation for the following tips, I share my classroom management secrets.

1. Have a sense of humor with the students. Be willing to laugh at yourself and with them, (however, never at them). The rapport you will build will eliminate behavior problems through friendship and understanding.

2. Have fair and consistent rules. Back them up with consequences that have teeth. My favorite consequence is lost recess. I have never found anything as effective. Additionally, be judicious. Do not allow a traditionally "good" student to be exempt from a consequence just because he/she rarely commits an infraction. **TREAT EVERYONE THE SAME.**

3. Reward, reward, reward and praise, praise, praise, but only when they deserve it. Reward and praise in over abundance has little to no significance. Students must know they have earned it. Students will strive for this type of praise and reward. It is a powerful motivater for excellence in academics and accountability in behavior.

4. Garner support from parents. When the teacher and parents work as a team, the student's achievement and accountability of his/her action increases. In essence, follow through at home by the parents and at the school from the teacher sends a powerful message to the student. "You are as responsible at home as at school and vice versus." Additionally, as stated earlier, never pass-up an opportunity to make a positive comment. A few kind word can work wonders.

5. Never give-up on a student. This can be very difficult at times. Constant and consistent attention can work miracles. Some students just need to know you care. A teacher that cares about his/her students will have a better teacher/student relationship. Rapport is everything.

6. Use your counselor, nurse, vice principal and principal effectively. This means, do not send a student to the counselor for every little thing. Keep them for the big issues: fighting, stealing, vandalism, harassment, etc. Attempt to handle as much as possible in class. In-class discipline is where many deals are cut and much improved behavior occurs. A student knows that he is accountable to the teacher, the person who is watching him/her the majority of the day. It is also easier to reward for improvement or discipline for digressions.

Your counselor is also a fertile resource for class lessons about conflict resolution, self concept/image, cultural awareness, etc. Ask them what they have to offer. Additionally, your nurse is also a resource not to be neglected. He/she can make sure your students are physically prepared to be top notch students. An unhealthy or sick child will never be a good student. The counselor and the nurse, if effective, responsive and supportive are two of the unsung heroes at most schools.

7. Please use my questions from chapter six (P. 42) when discussing an incident. Get the student to talk. **DO NOT LECTURE! THEY WILL JUST TUNE YOU OUT.**

8. When you have a supportive parent, call home and have the parent and the student involved in a three-way phone call. This is the next best thing to a parent/teacher/student conference.

9. Conduct parent/teacher conferences. Do not delay or feel it will not help. Many parents will back you. In many cases, their child's behavior is no surprise to them.

10. Follow through on consequences. Too many teachers say, "You'll be staying in at recess" and then forget. Keep lists on the board of who is accountable for what, whether it is homework or behavior related. Students miss nothing. If your consequences have no teeth or are not administered, poor behavior patterns will result.

In conclusion, I do not profess to have a classroom without discipline issues; however, I feel I have many less than other teachers. When I first started teaching, I was certain that my students would not like me because of my demanding presence and highly disciplined environment. It has been just the opposite. My students thrive and enjoy my demands and discipline. They want a consistent, well defined and stimulating environment where learning is priority one and the teacher will not accept substandard academics or behavior. It just feels good to do the right thing for a teacher who cares by demanding their best.

CHAPTER 19
FINANCES

You can never start saving too soon or too much for your retirement. As a teacher, you have an opportunity to save money for retirement through a Tax Sheltered Annuity (TSA) 403B. I recommend that you talk to your payroll office and find out which companies work with your school district. I will not go into all the details about a 403B. However, I hope the following facts will immediately motivate you to initiate a TSA 403B.

1. You can have up to 20% of your salary, after Social Security or State Teacher's Retirement Fund contribution, deducted from your paycheck. These monies are before **TAXES**. In essence, tax dollars, that would have gone to the state or federal governments, go into your TSA 403B and make you money. You'll pay taxes when you start to draw on the TSA 403B.

2. You can not get at this money (without paying a penalty) until you are 59.5 years old. This will keep you from dipping into it frivolously.

3. It is automatically deducted from your paycheck every month.

4. Depending on your TSA 403B provider, you can invest the monies in mutual funds. Traditionally, mutuals make on average about 12% per annum. That is not bad.

This final chapter has absolutely nothing to do with classroom management directly. However, if your finances are less than secure, it will effect one aspect or another in your classroom.

Get more information. A TSA 403B may be for you !